A BROAD CANVAS

Art in East Anglia since 1880

PARKE SUTTON PUBLISHING

Alfred Cohen *Lifeboat Café*, 1986
(previous page); H. H. La Thangue
Landscape Study, 1889 (opposite).

A BROAD CANVAS

Art in East Anglia since 1880

Ian Collins

PARKE SUTTON PUBLISHING

THIS BOOK is a study of how the landscapes
and spirit of a place have been absorbed
into a wide variety of art. It is a personal choice,
not a definitive guide. That so many fine artists
have been omitted or mentioned only briefly
should be taken as further proof of the peculiar
strength of creative talent in East Anglia.

Ian Collins, Norwich,
May 1990

TO MY PARENTS

A BROAD CANVAS
Published by Parke Sutton Publishing,
Magdalen House, 1 Bull Close Road, Norwich

Text copyright © 1990 Ian Collins
This edition copyright © 1990 Parke Sutton Publishing
ISBN 1-870337-06-9

Printed in England by Clays Ltd, St Ives plc

Typeset in Bembo and Berkeley Old Style

Francis Newbery *View from a Window, Walberswick*, 1912 (opposite); Lucien Pissarro *River Stour, Stratford St. Mary*, 1934 (top); Edward Bawden *Cattlemarket, Braintree*, 1937 (middle); Mary Newcomb *Rider on the Shingle*, 1987 (bottom).

A Broad Canvas

Contents

FOREWORD

Few of the artists brought together in this book are native to Norfolk, Suffolk and Essex, so what brought them to these counties? The popular answer is that they were influenced by those great native masters, John Crome, Thomas Gainsborough and John Constable. These cast their spell, of course, but it was one which the immigrant artists carefully avoided. My old friends Cedric Morris and John Nash were often asked if they had come to the Stour Valley in the 1930s to disprove Sickert's dismissal of its famous scenery as a 'sucked orange' — a question they found unanswerable. For to each of them the valley existed as though Constable had never been born. They, like so many other painters, had drifted to East Anglia during the agricultural depression when it was a quiet, remote and unfashionable area, although one with a clear but mysterious climate which had produced centuries of writers and craftsmen. Before the last war there were parts of Essex which could have been hundreds of miles from London and, as for north Norfolk, its remoteness was comparable to Northumberland in today's terms. There were few, if any, galleries, festivals or even good bookshops, and an artist living in his rented cottage or abandoned farmhouse was a colourful oddity. The small number of art schools in Britain meant that most trained artists knew each other, if only by name, and there were frequently deliberate attempts to create supportive coteries in certain villages and on the coast. Many painters came to work in East Anglia because Cornwall had become so crowded, and dominated by certain names. Suffolk and Norfolk in particular were in those days huge, spacious and yet rather lost places. They were also, in ordinary rural terms, poverty-stricken: one could exist there very cheaply in a stringent atmosphere which kept one 'on the go', as they said locally. It was an exceedingly beautiful and little-touched part of the country, and the changes that the latter half of the 20th century would bring were then quite un-imaginable.

To set up an art school — and a kind of French art school at that — in Dedham during the 1930s, as Cedric Morris and Arthur Lett-Haines did, was an act of provocation and daring. Not only did they have Constable on their very doorstep, but Alfred Munnings was also just round the corner. Its prospectus offered 'Instruction for the new forms and their recent development' for 26 guineas a year. An early pupil was the teenage Lucian Freud. When the East Anglian School of Painting and Drawing, as it was called, burnt to the ground, Munnings drove to and fro as it blazed, leaning out of his motor-car like Mr Toad and shouting 'Down with modern art!' This according to John Nash.

The School moved to Hadleigh and I was introduced to it in its heyday by the poet James Turner. It was summer and the pupils were at their easels in the famous iris garden. Sir Cedric was weeding and Lett was cooking, and the students (who were not referred to as such, but as artists in all 'degrees of efficiency') were working away in what was really an open-air *atelier* manner. The School was enchanting and by that time very famous. Witty, earthy, quite cut off from the Suffolk

Cedric Morris *Wartime Garden*,
1944, oil on canvas, 61 × 76cm.

I had been born into, what I was seeing was the last of the old forms of art teaching and also the last of Bohemia. The air reeked of garlic, wine, roses and strong tea. Being at that time a poet I was set to work composing catalogues. After this initiation, visits to Benton End became regular events, usually with John Nash, and he and Cedric would talk about gardening, not art. The gardening link between many of the East Anglian artists was a very important, learned and professional one and there was much flower painting. Cedric Morris's great garden oils had a brightness and ferocity which could shock, whilst John Nash's botanical drawings were filled with an intellectual understanding of plants. John's flower-painting classes at the Field Studies Centre at nearby Flatford Mill were always packed. Just before he set off to teach he would pick his 'models' from the garden, usually with a certain reluctance as if he couldn't bear to carry blooms away from it.

He and his wife Christine, a Slade girl to whom he had been introduced by Dora Carrington, first came to Wormingford, a Stour-side village, in 1929. There they rented cottages for their working holidays. All around them was spread the gloriously impacted ruin of the Constable family's river economy: the collapsed locks, the tangled towpaths and the Stour itself, dense with blooms, like the stream in Millais' *Ophelia*. This was the watery wilderness of my childhood in which cows stood belly-deep in meadowsweet and giant buttercups. In 1943, whilst working as a war artist once again, John bought an ancient, half-abandoned farmhouse called Bottengoms, a name straight out of Mervyn Peake. It was a sad time. A few years previously he had lost his small son in an accident; he also experienced a sense of *déjà vu* when, yet once more, he had to record fighting; and his close friend Eric Ravilious had just been killed. Ravilious and his wife, the artist Tirzah Garwood, lived a few miles from Wormingford at Castle Hedingham, near a little art colony known to John Nash as the 'Bard-field Boys'. These included Edward Bawden, John Aldridge and the mercurial Michael Ayrton. Bawden (who sometimes accompanied John Nash on painting holidays, memorably to Ironbridge, as I recall) was a native, having been born in Braintree. During the 1950s Great Bardfield became one long street of weavers, print-makers, writers, potters and artists of all kinds over which Edward Bawden and his wife Charlotte naturally presided.

My own late 1950s were spent in Aldeburgh writing novels and working for Benjamin Britten. The ecology was the very opposite to the Gainsborough-Constable countryside where I had been brought up. Marshes, seabirds, a crashing shore, minute flora and glittering flint. John Piper used to paint the exquisite medieval church architecture whilst his wife Myfanwy worked on the libretto for the *Turn of the Screw*. I remember the painter Mary Potter, who came to live at Aldeburgh in 1951, writing of it as a place which was associated with the storms, frustrations and tensions of creative necessity, as well as with its offered beauties, and she was right. Her Aldeburgh pictures correctly encapsulate its austerity. The first painting of hers which caught my imagination, and I think established our friendship, hung in Britten's house. It was of a white bird momentarily trapped in a walled garden when the light is failing. I still think of it, and to me it is as much a poem as a picture. Two other women artists, Peggy Somerville, who died in 1975, and Julia Laden, who now lives in Ipswich, also belong to my Aldeburgh period. Both superb colourists, their east Suffolk works in pastel especially pleased me and I was intrigued to see how such a hard-edged landscape could yield such soft depths in their hands. I have a painting of Peggy's which Julia gave me. It is of a thundery harvest field, the blackening sky turning the sheaves to fiery embers, and it reminds me how, as children, my brothers and I used to crawl into the prickly depths to escape a downpour. It also reminds me of the German artist Harry Becker who lived for the last two years of his life at Darsham, only a mile or two from where Peggy Somerville was eventually to have her studio. His totally uncompromising view of what was going on all around him on the poverty-stricken farms is such an eloquent reminder of how things were until 'just the other day'. Often too poor to buy canvas or drawing paper, Becker would use sized sacks from the fields, or bits of cardboard to paint on. He too had no inkling of what was coming — he died in 1928 — and his massive output reflects the traditional farm toil going on, slowly and penuriously, for ever.

Becker's father was a doctor who had emigrated to Colchester and, in his youth, the artist lived for a decade or so in The Minories, the fine house which has become one of East Anglia's most distinguished art galleries. During my teens The Minories was the family home of the Bensusan-Butts, who were related to the Pissarros. Lucien, Camille's son, often stayed there and painted in the garden. Going to tea at The Minories before it became a gallery, and going to parties there with John Nash after it had become Colchester's art centre, used to be thrilling events when I was young. An acacia which Lucien painted is still growing in the garden, and this charming Georgian residence, now squeezed by the corporation bus-park, makes a wonderfully direct connection with the Impressionists. It was through spending his childhood in this house that my old friend John Bensusan-Butt himself became an artist, for he said 'Living there, surrounded with pictures by Lucien and Camille, it was impossible not to have a colour sense and a desire to paint.' We once held a tremendous fancy-dress party there, all wearing 18th-century clothes, myself in a suit last worn by the explorer Captain Oates on a similar occasion.

The opening of art galleries throughout East Anglia after the war and the arrival of a new population which purchases works of art has transformed the situation for our local painters, sculptors and craftsmen. Nearly every market town now has an art gallery, as it does a festival. Gainsborough's birthplace in Sudbury, a prim hotel when I was small, has acquired an international reputation during its short life as a museum-cum-gallery for contemporary pictures, and there are first-rate commercial galleries from Kings Lynn to Thaxted. Civic art schools and art societies of all kinds continue to proliferate, and there is no 'Now' and 'Then'. Nor, stylistically, can there be said to be any obvious East Anglian tradition. The scene is one of a conscious endeavour to be rooted in a bit of England that all the artists working here, whether born in these counties or not, have discovered to be still wonderfully fertile ground were painting is concerned. Or indeed writing, if it comes to that. Many artists live where they do for a mixture of economic and social reasons and, by painting what is near at hand, almost unconsciously make themselves the 'explainers' of a particular village or piece of marshland, or their inhabitants. I cannot remember visiting any artist-friend without recognising that I was stepping into his vision, as it were. And then, for a writer, there is always the fascinating thing known as 'association' — the touching of a great past.

There are small personal coincidences, too, which are of little interest to anyone other than oneself, such as finding out that Beatrix Potter sat painting watercolours in the lane leading to Brundon Mill where my brothers and I played as children. Or, having been sent on long Sunday afternoon walks by our parents through the high-up Cornard lanes, that the young Gainsborough painted one of the world's best landscapes, *Cornard Wood*, there. As to why a writer should gravitate so positively towards painters it is now hard to say. The truth is that their friendships and way of local life came first, and very early on, in my own creative experience. The influences of poets and novelists were to follow. Some years ago I had to select some of William Hazlitt's essays for a volume in the Penguin English Library and there, in his *On the Pleasure of Painting*, was the perfect apology for a writer's involvement in art. Hazlitt was a mediocre painter who became a brilliant writer, a transition which did not make him at all grateful.

There is a pleasure in painting which none but painters know. In writing you have to contend with the world; in painting, you have only to carry on a friendly strife with nature. You sit down to your task, and are happy. From the moment that you take up the pencil, and look Nature in the face, you are at peace with your own heart.

So maybe that is it.

RONALD BLYTHE

INTRODUCTION

Since the eighteenth century East Anglia has been a major source of inspiration for the art of painting. This is surprising as it is not conventionally beautiful. For the artist working in the late eighteenth or early nineteenth century East Anglia did not in any obvious way satisfy contemporary taste; unlike the Lake District or the mountain areas of Wales and Scotland it did not invite sublime associations, and its lack of variety left unfulfilled even the desire for the picturesque. By the aesthetic standards of the period it seemed a relatively mundane, agricultural landscape and was still then a comparatively poor area. It is only since Constable and Crome that its unassertive beauty has been appreciated, for owing to the art it has produced we have nowadays learnt to see it as if through artists' eyes.

What turned the key to its magic was the recognition of its similarity to Holland. In the seventeenth century the major revelation in landscape painting had been the discovery of visual beauty in the undramatic, unclassical lands of northern Europe. Thomas Gainsborough is often quoted as saying, when much in demand as a fashionable portrait painter, that he yearned to get back to his first love, of painting the Suffolk landscape. Although he brought to his depiction of it fresh perceptions, his famous *Cornard Wood* owes much to the example of the Dutch artist, Jacob van Ruisdael, whose work hung in the homes of certain East Anglian collectors. When at the end of his life Gainsborough virtually abandoned portraiture for landscape, he did not, however, return to the fresh immediacy of his early Suffolk

Thomas Gainsborough *Landscape with a View of Cornard Village*, c. 1750, oil on canvas, 76 × 151cm.

scenes but, in keeping with his late style, painted sweet pastoral evocations in a fanciful, Italianate manner. Nevertheless it was Gainsborough's conviction in painting the immediate landscape that gave Constable the confidence to paint his native countryside, to conclude 'there is room enough for a natural painter'. Paradoxically, Constable's decision — to break away from orthodox formulae — resulted in landscapes which to a twentieth-century eye appear the most conventional in their representation of East Anglia. Yet Constable is arguably the most revolutionary of all British artists.

'These scenes', he wrote of East Bergholt and the River Stour, 'made me a painter, and I am grateful.' This despite the fact that as a painter he endured much ridicule and relied for support on a handful of close friends. Reading his letters, one is reminded of Van Gogh: there is the same absolute conviction in his work, the same religious intensity and the same humility in front of nature — a sense of wonder which he strives to capture against all odds, for these letters also reveal self-doubt, anxiety and moods of depression.

Constable far outreached his contemporaries in the rendering of light and atmosphere. He had admired Rubens' *Château de Steen* in Sir George Beaumont's collection, especially his treatment of 'dewy light and freshness, the departing shower with the exhilaration of returning sun'. Constable himself remains unsurpassed in portraying the lucidity of sunlight after rain or the sparkle of leaves rustled by the wind. It was sensations like these that, for Constable, brought the Suffolk landscape to life and made it lived in. His paintings offer the pastoral experience of one who knew the landscape intimately. They are also peopled by those who labour on the land. We do not find in his art the sweeping vista of magnificent scenic effects, neither mountains nor classical ruins. There is no grand overall conception but a record of intimate individual responses: the Protestant not the Catholic view.

Constable's remarkable achievement had no immediate following, its legacy being confined in Britain to his family and one or two isolated admirers such as Thomas Creswick. But his discoveries provided a revelation when his paintings were exhibited in France. So great was the interest in his work that Ackerman's set up a Constable room in their gallery in Paris. It was in part owing to his example that artists settled in the village of Barbizon in order to paint a landscape that is not unlike the woods of East Anglia. This development led directly to the emergence of Impressionism which carried Constable's experiments in portraying effects of light to their chromatic conclusion. It is perhaps significant that the man who assimilated Impressionism and took it further into a more expressionist mode — Van Gogh — began as a painter of the landscape of his native Holland, which had in effect provided that roots of Constable's art.

In the twentieth century Mary Potter is one of the few artists who has been able to add a new dimension to Constable's portrayal of Suffolk light, with her sharply felt but gently handled evocations of the light she experienced at Aldeburgh. She painted in oils and in water-colour, in a similar style with both media. Her opalescent tones encourage one again to see landscape through the eyes of an artist, to register the suffusing light of East Anglia in terms of her muted har-monies. The wide open spaces of East Anglia give the sky unusual prominence, whilst its light is reflected off sea, river or fen. Even where there is no water the light seems brushed into the leaves and grasses and shines up again from a road still wet after rain.

It is difficult to explain why East Anglia, and in particular Norwich, became such an outstanding centre for watercolour painting during the nineteenth century and helped to make the English water-colour tradition internationally renowned. Rather like the landscape, the medium was regarded as aesthetically second-rate in the late eighteenth century. It was then used primarily as a sketching tool, a means of preparing an artist for work in oils. A painter could not become a Royal Academician if he only painted in watercolour. Its second-class status may explain why those artists who became interested in it felt more room to experiment. The speed at which they did so, the closeness of their contacts, the competitiveness of their spirit and the intensity of their ambition add up to an extraordinary story which included many great names — Robert Cozens, Thomas Girtin, J.M.W. Turner and J.S. Cotman, among others.

Cotman must rank as one of the greatest of all East Anglian artists, even though much of his finest work was done elsewhere, in London and Yorkshire. He left Norwich for London in order to develop his art, believing that London was the air that artists should breathe. He began, as other artists did, to frequent the home of Dr Thomas Monro, the physician to the Bethlem Hospital and expert on respiratory diseases who had inherited the unfinished work of Cozens, one of the greatest eighteenth-century watercolourists, and who employed artists to finish or do their own versions of Cozens's original ideas. It is probable that the Sketching Club, begun by Thomas Girtin and others in 1799, grew out of the evening gatherings at Dr Monro's for he was a great patron of watercolourists and also provided an inspirational focus for them. The Norwich Society of Artists, founded in 1803, imitated the collective identity which the Sketching Club in London had fostered. It held evening meetings once a fortnight, put on exhibitions and organised sketching parties. In its early years the dominant artists were John Crome, Robert Ladbrooke, Robert Dixon, John Thirtle and Charles Hodgson, but when Cotman returned to Norwich in 1806, his ambitions frustrated, he joined this Society, exhibited for the first time in 1807 and made his presence immediately felt. His influence was most noticeable in the work of Dixon and Thirtle.

Cotman had returned to Norwich to make his living as a drawing master ('the one thing I most dreaded on setting out in life') and as an antiquarian illustrator. He had shown a mastery of the medium in his earliest watercolours, in which atmospheric effects are created through the grading of washes. But in 1803, and in the two succeeding years, he had made visits to Yorkshire at the invitation of Mr and Mrs Cholmeley of Brandsby Hall, and there he developed a more classical approach to watercolour in his paintings of the Greta valley. The technique he developed no longer built up tone and hue through overlapping, carefully graded washes, but instead allowed each wash to retain a clear edge, the composition being built up out of

John Constable *Golding Constable's Kitchen Garden*, 1815, oil on canvas, 33 × 51cm (opposite).

John Sell Cotman *Mousehold Heath, Norwich*, c. 1810, watercolour, 30 × 46cm (right).

interconnecting negative and positive shapes that convey space and light within a brilliantly conceived formal composition. In this way Cotman brought a new dimension to the art of watercolour painting, which enabled him to express surprising riches of feeling with even such humble subjects as a drop-gate or an untidy bank at the edge of a stream. These extraordinary watercolours, which seem modern even today, were so unconventional at the time that they achieved no popularity and Cotman, convinced of his achievement, became extremely disillusioned, gloom and despair alternating with periods of intense activity.

After his marriage in 1809, Cotman took on an increased number of pupils. He also established a circulating library of drawings which subscribers could borrow and copy. Then, in 1812, he accepted the post of drawing master to the banker and antiquarian, Dawson Turner — a job that required him to leave Norwich for Yarmouth, where he lived until 1823. For Dawson Turner he produced many drawings of ancient buildings in Norfolk. He also helped research and illustrate *Architectural Antiquities of Normandy* for which Dawson Turner wrote the text. Much of Cotman's architectural work is, if compared with his earlier watercolours, pedestrian. Realisation of this may have contributed to those bouts of depression that left him speechless for weeks on end. Nevertheless he struggled on to establish himself as a professional artist. Inspired also by Turner's readiness to experiment, Cotman developed a new paste technique which gives to his dramatic swirls in watercolour the appearance of oils.

Cotman, though he painted comparatively few East Anglian scenes, has become the quintessential East Anglian artist largely due to the fact that the best collection of his work is enshrined in the Castle Museum, Norwich. He still remains one of the main artistic inspirations to artists working in the region: even the collagist, Francis

Davison, whose work superficially looks far removed from Cotman's, was greatly influenced by him and knew intimately the works on display in Norwich. In Davison's case, it was Cotman's powerful sense of pictorial composition combined with natural grace that impressed.

If Cotman dominates any account of East Anglian art, his impact was slightly preceded by that of John Crome, who remained an influential figure within the Norwich School until his death in 1821. Within the history of British art Crome remains a rare phenomenon: an artist of national stature without national ambitions. Unlike Cotman, he was content to stay in Norwich though his remarkable ability would have allowed him to take London by storm. He was a superb technician, both in oils and watercolour, and had studied closely the great landscape painters of Holland and the Netherlands. Their influence is felt in Crome's choice of subject matter: townscapes, night scenes and village views. But he was no mere imitator. His paintings spring from an authenticity of response to what he saw; some are startlingly original in the freshness of their viewpoint, in their disregard for pictorial conventions. But although Crome was bold enough to work directly with the landscape around him, he was, unlike Constable, not a revolutionary. His temperament was, as his many friends repeatedly attest in their correspondence, modest, gentle and full of charm. And it is these qualities which also pervade his work. His aim was a unified grasp of the whole, as he admits in an oft-quoted letter to John Stark: 'trifles in nature must be overlooked that we· may have our feelings raised by seeing the whole picture at a glance, not knowing how or why we are so charmed'.

At his best Crome's work sustains a powerful sense of balance, not just between previous traditions and direct observation, but also between the different pictorial elements in his work. His etchings, which — like all he did — are remarkable for their technical dexterity

John Crome *Moonrise on the Yare*, c. 1811–16, oil on canvas, 71 × 111cm (left).

Henry Bright *Remains of St. Benedict's Abbey on the Norfolk Marshes – Thunderstorm Clearing*, 1847, oil on canvas, 80 × 133cm (opposite).

and subtlety, rely for their impact on an extraordinary balance between light and dark areas, often contained within one complex bare tree, its branches dark against the sky and light against the undergrowth beneath. It was Crome who, by staying in Norwich and being by all accounts such an exceptionally nice fellow, welcome in every household at all levels of society, established virtually single-handed the Norwich School. Though the art world was then small in London, it was even smaller in Norwich and almost every painter of that period in Norwich either trained under Crome or knew him and his work. As Camille Pissarro was to the Impressionists, so Crome became the father figure of the Norwich School. His best work invites comparison with that of Corot in its aspiration towards stillness and calm beauty.

A considerable number of more journeyman artists, some of them — like Thomas Middleton — exceptionally talented, were able to sustain lifelong careers producing paintings for the middle classes of Norwich in the nineteenth century. Middleton himself died young, in his thirtieth year, but the watercolours he produced on first reaching maturity make bold play with the white of the paper and in their use of the watercolour medium have a purity reminiscent of Cotman. Middleton's name is often linked with that of his friend, Henry Bright, who likewise learnt from Cotman — in particular from his chalk drawings of the 1830s, Bright having taken lessons from Cotman as well as from Crome's son, John Berney Crome. Bright's inventiveness

with watercolour, which he mixed with other media, led him to develop a sometimes dazzling capacity for virtuoso display. He also travelled widely and, aware of his market, occasionally resorted in his later years to predictable views. Middleton, Bright, Robert Leman, Thomas Lound and other artists sustained the tradition of the Norwich School, with its dedication to ordinary scenes, into the middle of the nineteenth century — though if compared with Cotman all were aesthetically less ambitious. It was not until the twentieth century loomed — and modern art was starting to fragment the practice and manner of painting — that East Anglia suddenly and surprisingly once again provided inspiration to artists. And it is the rich diversity of this continuing story, with its many interconnecting links, that Ian Collins here recounts.

Frances Spalding

The north Norfolk coast, curving from the estuary of the Great Ouse to the Yare's mouth, holds a shaky line between land and water. Bits of shore are forever toppling into the sea, giving a foretaste, perhaps, of future floods. Many painters have worked and wandered here – relishing a sense of being on the edge and the curious fact that, however clouded the day, the light tends to be vivid and the sun appears in a flaming farewell at sunset. Moreover, there is wild variety to this landscape which is far removed from the flat sameness claimed by Noël Coward. Above King's Lynn a band of chalk surfaces in low cliffs, while salt-marshes, covered in sea lavender and sliced by creeks and channels, stretch from Blakeney to Cley. Further on, past the Victorian resorts of Sheringham and Cromer, and the 'Poppyland' relics of Sidestrand and Overstrand, a strip of caravan-studded sand and dune runs almost clear to Yarmouth.

For painters and other visitors this is a place of bracing holidays, hideaways and hospital stays. Since the journalist Clement Scott wrote more than a century ago about the Great Eastern Railway Company's new line to the north Norfolk coast – and launched a stampede towards the flowered lanes of Poppyland – the area's remoteness has been increasingly patchy. But here remain some of the finest views and least-trodden paths in East Anglia.

One man who knew every track across the saltmarshes at Wells-next-the-Sea was **Frank Southgate** (1872-1916). Marching over his favourite habitat, he wore a uniform of old oilskins and went armed with a sketchbook and gun. Ornithology, drawing and wildfowling were the passions of his short life. On one occasion he despatched 203 small wading birds with a single blast from a punt gun; yet his pictures of flocks in flight could be lyrical. The naturalist Peter Scott said that Southgate was 'the first bird painter in this country to introduce a freedom of technique, even an impressionist technique, to the painting of birds'.

Edward Frank Southgate, the son of a Hunstanton postmaster, showed an early aptitude for adventure: a friend once held his feet while he dangled over a cliff in search of sandmartins' eggs. He

SOME ENCHANTMENT lies upon the coast of north Norfolk which leaves it in memory, not just an impression of peculiar beauty, but a series of pictures standing out as vividly as if you had opened a book.

(Lilias Rider Haggard,
Eastern Daily Press, August 1938)

Hayward Young *The Charm of Poppyland*. **Illustrated in the Great Eastern Railway Magazine collected edition of 1914, and used as a poster.**

received his art training in Cambridge and Perth, and then in London – first at the Slade and later under Arthur Cope RA. In 1903, when launched as a professional painter, he married Ethel Winlove, from his home town. The couple settled in a new house, Wingate, at Wells, where Frank established a pattern of painting in the summer and contracting 'goose fever' each winter. Between October and March, sketching was fitted into a wildfowler's waiting hours. But the kill was all. If he returned home empty-handed, he wept.

In those Edwardian autumns, the night sky around Wells and Holkham was alive with a rush of birds from the north: waders and wigeon, brent, pink-footed and white-fronted geese. They attracted a brave and hardy band of sportsmen, of whom none was more obsessed than Southgate. On moonlit nights he would dig himself into the mud, to await – as frost crusted his eyelashes – the dawn flight. Many goose hunts ended in forced marches across the saltings to beat the tide.

Early pictures (sometimes signed E. F. Southgate, or E. Frank Southgate) were stilted. The artist seems to have drawn in his studio from stuffed birds, mounted or hanging on wires, and from photographs. But the mature work became infused with its maker's love of wild places and growing knowledge of bird movements. Particularly in watercolour, he was to combine both great freedom in rendering backgrounds and skilled handling of pigment with a naturalist's precision in drawing his subjects. But, ever a wildfowler at heart, he spurned sentimentality in his art: some birds are seen falling prey to a natural predator, still more to a gun. Southgate was a regular contributor to *Illustrated Sporting and Dramatic News*, and he also collaborated on several natural history and travel books; exhibiting widely, he was elected a member of the Royal Society of British Artists, in 1905.

When the Great War broke out, Southgate joined the Sportman's Battalion of the Royal Fusiliers – even though, at 42, he seemed too old for such a

Frank Southgate, photographed in about 1910 (above) and (below) Southgate's *Curlews Feeding*, 1908, watercolour, 35 × 56cm.

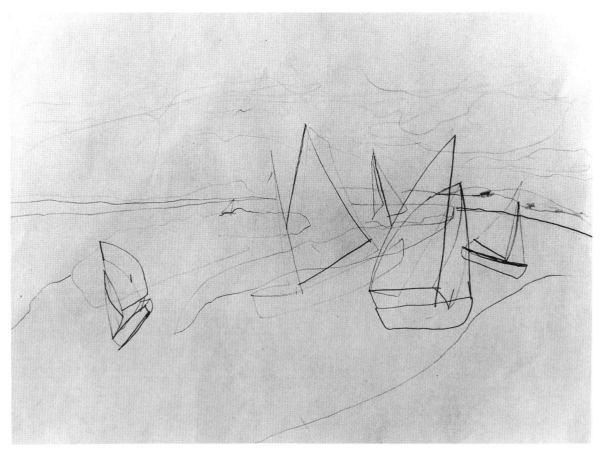

Ben Nicholson *Burnham Overy Staithe*, 1969, pencil.

wild goose chase. But he was fortified by bleak humour as, 50 years later, one of his Norfolk comrades recalled. 'He would joke about the hopelessness of our position, wallowing as we were, in mud to our middles, if a German raiding party should jump into our trench', wrote Pat Cringle. 'He would laugh after intently watching an object in the darkness, quite convinced that it was crawling to the attack, until an exploding Verey light would reveal it as an inoffensive post. "Just as", he'd say, "in the old days we'd watch for duck on the marshes . . . our eyes fixed on some darker patch of darkness. Surely a swimming duck? No – the moon cleared the cloud and it was just another patch of mud."' Spirit was not enough, however. Frank Southgate died of heart failure in February 1916, after running two miles to a front-line position. He is buried in northern France and commemorated on a plaque to the war dead in Wells church.

A mile or two from Wells, across the sweep of Holkham bay, the artist Matthew Smith and his wife, the Slade-trained painter Gwen Salmond, owned Ship House, Burnham Overy Staithe, between 1933 and 1955. Smith worked from a studio in the yard, but spent most of his time in London and Provence. It was Mrs Smith who loved to escape to north Norfolk and she who was at Ship House when news came through that both their sons had been killed in action

in the Royal Air Force. **Ben Nicholson** (1894-1982) followed John Piper in recording the Palladian splendour of Holkham Hall, and drew skimming yachts at Overy Staithe while staying with Lord and Lady Zuckerman at Burnham Thorpe. Nicholson, Barbara Hepworth, Ivon Hitchens and Henry and Irina Moore spent one holiday at Happisburgh in 1931.

But **Henry Moore** (1898-1986) already knew this coastline well. In 1922 his family had moved from Castleford, due to the declining health of his ex-miner father. Moore's sister, Mary, gave up her post as headmistress of a large primary school in Yorkshire to take over the 50-pupil school at Wighton, set amid rolling fields and pure air near Wells. But within a month of arrival, Raymond Moore died, and was buried in Wighton churchyard. Mary ran the village school for three years, and during that time Henry, a student at the Royal College of Art, was a vacation visitor. Doubtless to the consternation of passers-by, he used to work on blocks of stone in the yard of the brick-and-flint schoolhouse, steadying them between his feet or lodging them in the ground. A faded photograph shows the young sculptor in shirt sleeves and braces carving a dog, in Portland stone, and in the background his first 'mother and child' is visible. Also in the scene is a piece of white marble from which a head and shoulders are emerging. When the subsequent owners of Wighton schoolhouse – painter Alfred Cohen and his wife Diana – were clearing the garden in the early 1980s, they found the unfinished sculpture. It was returned to Moore before he died.

Besides being a congenial place for family reunions, north Norfolk had a lasting impact on Henry Moore's sculpture. It was here that he began to collect the chunks of flint which abound along the edges of lanes and fields; their twisted shapes were prototypes for future works of art. He visited his sister, Betty, whose husband taught at Mulbarton, near Norwich, and his brother, Raymond, a headmaster at Stoke Ferry. But Wighton was his first love. After Mary married bank employee George Garrould in 1925 and

moved to Wells, and then to Colchester 18 months later, things were never the same. Writing to fellow student Edna Ginesi, from Mulbarton in the summer of 1925, Moore said: 'In Wighton . . . I had meals how & when I liked & had a large stock of stones in the back garden and mucked up the premises as much as I liked – I can't be as selfish as I was then, but I'm thankful I'm not having to spend my holidays in London as I thought I might be obliged to do – I'm thankful for these two spots in Norfolk where I can sit in the open air, crosslegged on patches of grass & chip stone – though I was nearly sent loopy this afternoon by the incessant lowing of a cow that the farmer next door is starving for killing.'

That same summer, from Wells, Moore wrote to another student friend, Raymond Coxon, that if he had money he would make for 'a country district in England, somewhere like Wighton or Walsingham, and stay there until I'd found and wedded one of those richly formed, big-limbed, fresh faced, full

THE PANTILES and flint-encrusted façades of traditional north Norfolk shops have inspired a bold and brightly coloured array of oils, watercolours, pastels and silk-screened prints by the Chicago-born painter **Alfred Cohen** (b. 1920) who has lived at Wighton since 1978. He has also seized with delight on Cromer's now-closed Lifeboat Cafe, which he found to be a sea-side kaleidoscope, advertising its charms in gaudy chalks.

After a war-time spell as a US Air Force captain, serving in the South Pacific, Alfred Cohen became an American in Paris, where he studied painting and was heavily influenced by contemporary French art. He moved to England in 1960 and, after depicting the Channel ports, gravitated towards the Norfolk coast. Here he has developed his talent for print-making, while continuing to paint, primarily in oils.

All of his work – covering landscapes, interiors, still lifes and flower pieces – glows with wit, exuberance and affection. He loves the sort of scene that is decked out for a festival or celebration and his pictures are like a series of brilliant postcards home.

Part of Henry Moore's flint collection, begun with finds from Norfolk (below) and Moore, with *Reclining Figure*, 1929, brown hornton stone, 56 × 84 × 38cm.

Alfred Cohen *Lifeboat Café*, 1986, oil on board, 51 × 61cm (left).

blooded country wenches, built for breeding, honest, simple minded, practical, common sensed, healthily sexed lasses that I've seen about here.' Here were the inspirations for an array of reclining figures.

A later link with East Anglia was provided by the Norwich-born sculptor Bernard Meadows, who was Moore's studio assistant in the late 1930s. Chiefly, however, the connection survives in the work. Four large bronzes can be seen in college courts at Cambridge; drawings and sculptures are on view at the Sainsbury Centre, on the Norwich campus of the University of East Anglia. And there is a splendid Madonna in St Mary's Church, Barham, outside Ipswich, which was commissioned by Sir Jasper Ridley of nearby Mockbeggars Hall as a memorial to his son and three other Claydon villagers who were killed in the Second World War.

While Moore was staying in Wells, another artist was succumbing to consumption, further along the coast. **Francis Sydney Unwin** (1885-1925) – a Dorset-born draughtsman, etcher and lithographer of architectural subjects and landscapes – had trained at London's Slade School of Fine Art, travelled widely and exhibited with the New English Art Club from

THE WATERCOLOURIST **Gerald Ackermann** (1876-1960) painted castles and cathedrals throughout the country; but, after settling at Blakeney, he also marvelled at the immense architecture of a north Norfolk sky.

Gerald Ackermann *Fair at Blakeney*, pencil and watercolour, 25 × 37cm.

Born Arthur Gerald Ackermann, in Blackheath, this art dealer's son was a prize-winning student at the Royal Academy Schools. He exhibited widely and was elected a member of the Royal Institute of Painters in Water-colours in 1912. During the First World War he served with the Artists' Rifles – a photograph in the *Daily Sketch*, on 14th October 1915, pictured him practising with a mock machine-gun.

Ackermann held that watercolour landscapes should be 'pure, transparent and direct'. Speed and simplicity were essential. But preparation was intense. At new painting sites he liked to spend several days with his sketchbook, jotting down pencil and crayon details of composition and colour. Once a suitable subject had been selected, he would visit it at all hours, to find the best 'effect'. He might make a dozen quick notes of cloud formations. Stormy days – 'Constable days', with skies racing overhead – were judged ideal. 'The moving shadows travelling across your landscape enable you to mass your light and shade', he advised. 'The mere topography is not of much account.'

Final pictures – never more than 35 by 25 centimetres – were completed outdoors in single sittings. Ackermann wrote: 'What a studio picture may gain in design and draughtsmanship, it will surely lose in that vitality which is only to be obtained by working on the spot.'

1913. He was admired by other artists and was friendly with John and Christine Nash, who were for a time his neighbours in Buckinghamshire. In late lithographs, drawn in chalk, pen and wash, he depicted the buildings and skyline of Cromer. As Campbell Dodgson wrote in a posthumous tribute, published in 1926: 'Unwin was never a colourist; he saw nature, or rather he recorded his impressions of nature, in black and white, or in monochrome washes of grey, brown or blue. His tendency was towards a severe style: if he chose an architectural subject, he laid emphasis on firm outlines and deep shadows, and aimed at producing an effect of weight and mass.'

But in 1916 tuberculosis was diagnosed, and Unwin spent five months in the private sanatorium at Mundesley (now extended and run as a rehabilitation

Francis Unwin *Cromer Hotels*, **1922, pencil and watercolour, 45 × 55cm (opposite page, top) and nearby Mundesley Hospital today (left). This view remains much as Unwin would have known it.**

A NEIGHBOUR of Philip Wilson Steer, in Cheyne Walk, Chelsea, was the painter and teacher **Walter Wesley Russell** (1867-1949). Like Steer, he explored a personal response to French Impressionism during painting holidays along the Suffolk coast. But north Norfolk was to provide him with a still greater wealth of subjects.

Russell, born in Epping, exhibited his first north Norfolk paintings at the Royal Academy as late as 1926. His sketchbooks, however, show that he had been visiting the area from the 1890s. He drew church-centred views from Stiffkey to Salthouse, and seaside scenes from West Runton to Cromer. In fresh and vivid oil studies on panel he captured the glory of late Victorian and Edwardian holidays, when the Empress Elizabeth of Austria was among those travelling to Cromer to take the air and to dip decorously into the North Sea. In 1910, *The Studio* magazine applauded Russell's 'lyric sentiment' and added that recent pictures displayed 'not only his true sense of colour, his skill as a draughtsman, the charm and refinement of his vision, but also the solemn inspiration and the profound poetry of his conception of and communion with Nature's grandeur.'

This book-binder's son left the Westminster School of Art in 1891 to work as an illustrator and etcher. He exhibited with the New English Art Club from 1893, and taught at the Slade from 1895 to 1927. A noted portraitist – influencing William Orpen and Augustus John – he married his model, Lydia Buston, in 1900. Despite an early attraction, Sickert's Fitzroy Street Group proved too radical for his taste, and he became increasingly an establishment figure. Exhibiting at the RA from 1898, he was elected a Royal Academician in 1926, serving as keeper from 1927 to 1942. He was knighted in 1935.

Walter Wesley Russell *Beach Scene, East Runton*, **oil on board, 14 × 23cm.**

centre). Set amid wooded grounds, a mile from the sea, the hospital was judged a tonic for TB sufferers in the last decades before curative drugs. Francis Unwin was released after treatment, but a remission proved temporary. In 1925 – a year in which Norfolk recorded 444 new tuberculosis cases and 251 fatalities – he died at Mundesley. The British Museum received a near-complete set of his etchings. John and Christine Nash (the latter a frequent visitor during his final illness) inherited his car and a quantity of furniture. His will had been witnessed by two patients at Mundesley; one was the painter Mark Gertler.

Born into East End poverty, in an enclosed community of Jewish refugees from Eastern Europe, **Mark Gertler** (1891-1939) was a mature painter before the age of 20. Having attended art classes at the Regent Street Polytechnic from 1906, begun an

Mark Gertler *Dorothy Morland,* **1937, oil on canvas, 69 × 56cm.**

apprenticeship at a stained-glass works, and been loaded with prizes at the Slade, he was soon recognised as a prodigious talent. Switching from starkly realistic portraits of his family, he introduced a semi-Cubist style into landscape, figure and still life studies; and completed his masterly attack on military madness, the *Merry-Go-Round*, in 1916. He drove himself hard, not least in a Bohemian social life, dancing on table-tops and entertaining rich art patrons like Lady Ottoline Morrell with stories and impromptu cabaret turns. 'There has seldom been a more exciting personality than he was when young,' the barrister St John Hutchinson recalled in 1940, 'with amazing gifts of draughtsmanship, amazing vitality and sense of humour and of mimicry unique to himself – a shock of hair, the vivid eyes of genius and consumption . . .'

Tuberculosis, confirmed in 1920, forced long stays in sanatoria. Grime, poverty, over-exertion – and perhaps the sense of dislocation that some detect in his work – had ruined his constitution. His mental state, always brittle in private, was further weakened by financial worries and frustrated love for the painter Dora Carrington. In September 1925 Gertler arrived at Mundesley after coughing up blood at a London dinner party. His condition proved less serious than he had feared. Soon he was writing to his literary tutor S. S. Koteliansky:

24 September 1925 Mundesley

My dear Kot . . . My future seems dreadful to me. What with this pernicious disease hanging over me, and a still great uncertainty about money . . .

I continue to get well. Why? Because the life is regular and I am kept away from nervous exhaustion and strain. Strangely enough, boredom does not seem to do one harm physically. I am sure that when I get back to London, I could continue to improve myself as well as anywhere in my own rooms, provided I live quietly and regularly.

There is an artist here called Unwin . . . He is in a poor way. Like myself he has had it for a second time, but *his* second attack was a dreadful affair. He has been in bed since last February. Think of it. The germ has attacked his heart and stomach. He will have to be in bed for another three months at least . . . He is not exactly a happy spectacle. But I feel I must go and see him, as it must be indescribably horrible to be in bed so long with no friends near by. He is a nice man, forty years old and very broken.

I am working from 2 to 4 and that makes a great difference.

At Mundesley Gertler completed at least one painting of the local landscape and basked in good wishes from Dora Carrington. It was fortunate that his specialist, Dr Andrew Morland, already admired his work – and the pair struck up a firm friendship.

Gertler persuaded Morland to travel to Italy, to confirm that an old chum, the novelist D. H. Lawrence, had TB. The doctor and his wife, Dorothy, had Gertler to stay with them at Mundesley at least twice, in 1930 and 1938, and they in turn became regular attenders at his Thursday social evenings in Hampstead. They acquired his picture *Sanatorium Garden in Norfolk*, and in 1937 Gertler painted a portrait of Dorothy Morland wearing a mantilla.

But, despite the support of friends, the artist remained prone to bouts of crippling depression. He wrote to Koteliansky, shortly before leaving the sanatorium:

30 November 1925   Mundesley
My dear Kot . . . In spite of my approaching release, I had a fit of the glooms recently . . . there were moments when I felt I must pack up and run away . . . This mood of super depression was brought on by several events. First Unwin died a few days ago, and the day before his death he sent for me to witness his will. He *would* not have anyone but me and one man (patient) I would choose to bring. Previous to this I hadn't seen him for ten days, and the change for the worse was so marked that I was profoundly shocked and depressed, and knew he was done for. Then the weather has been terrible – Siberia not in it – so we have been unable to do our walks

and consequently our routine is disorganised. And we depend entirely on routine for the passing of time . . .

Suffering from migraines, persisting money troubles and fears of a recurrence of illness, Gertler

Mark Gertler in 1923, two years before his first stay at Mundesley (left), and his painting *The Window*, oil on canvas, 1936, 30 × 41cm (below).

produced melancholic landscapes in the 1920s. In July 1929 he was back at Mundesley, but his TB was declared cured. 'My breakdown this time was entirely mental strain', he concluded. The following year he married the Slade-trained artist Marjorie Hodgkinson in France, but the struggle for health and cash continued to drain him. And he fretted over the quality of his work, which was now dominated by claustrophobic still lifes and Renoir-influenced nudes in sometimes garish colours. Most of the later landscapes were an invalid's view through windows.

In the summer of 1936 Gertler collapsed once more, and was again admitted to Mundesley. The following day he wrote to his friend, the publisher Thomas Balston.

2 July 1936   The Sanatorium, Mundesley, Norfolk
My dear Tom . . . I have been so unhappy at home

that I longed for *any* change and, when I got here, I went through the usual fit of depression this place always gives me on arrival. But I soon got over it, and now feel thankful for the peace and rest, which I have not been able to enjoy for months and months.

I have a beautiful room (all modern), large open window looking onto a good landscape which I hope to paint as soon as I feel up to it. For the time being they are keeping me in bed for 'observation'. It is very tedious, but I'm not opposing it because I do really feel very weak still. I have been examined a good deal here already, but so far they are not able to discover any trace of real activity, and therefore our trip abroad is not threatened.

But shortly afterwards, Gertler cut his throat and a vein in an arm – then summoned a nurse. He was watched continuously for several weeks. Marjorie

Claughton Pellew-Harvey
Embankment at Night, **1920, ink, pastel, gouache and watercolour, 45 × 60cm.**

was often at his bedside, having booked herself into a nearby hotel. Slowly, in the ordered regime of the sanatorium, calm returned. At some point, perhaps on a tour of the local countryside, Gertler painted a scene at Hautbois, near Coltishall. In October he returned to London.

Things were no better, however. In 1939 a crisis was reached with the failure of an exhibition at the Lefevre Gallery and the growing certainty of war. Andrew Morland was called in early June: Gertler had taken an overdose and turned on the gas, then turned it off again. Later that month he did not have second thoughts. Dr Morland found his body in his gas-filled studio. A post-mortem showed the old tuberculosis completely healed.

Another artist friend of Francis Unwin took lodgings at Mundesley, following childhood holidays in Norfolk and studies at the Slade. **Claughton Pellew-Harvey** (1890-1966), the son of a Cornish mining engineer, had been raised in Canada and London and was to help several contemporary painters achieve future fame, while hugging his own obscurity. The shy figure clung ever more tightly to cut-off north-east Norfolk after suffering great hardships, during detention in work camps in Scotland, Yorkshire and Dartmoor, as a conscientious objector to the First World War.

In his autobiography, **Paul Nash** (1889-1946) describes his first impressions of Claughton Pellew: 'Among the few people at the Slade who seemed in

Paul Nash *The Cliff to the North,* **pen, ink and wash, 39 × 30cm.**

the least interested in what I was doing was a slight dark man with a strange voice . . . the first creature of a truly poetic cast of mind I had met . . . His own work was remarkable for a searching intensity both in thought and execution.' Nash, who was to become a revolutionary war and landscape artist, credits Pellew with having fired his feeling for nature: 'I found he had a deep love for the country, particularly for certain of its features, such as ricks and stooks of corn. At first I was unable to understand an almost devotional approach to a hay stack, and listened doubtfully to a rhapsody on the beauty of its form. Such objects, and, indeed, the whole organic life of the countryside were still, for me, only the properties and scenes of my "visions". Slowly, however, the individual beauty of certain things, trees particularly, began to dawn upon me.' In November 1912, Nash stayed with his friend at Mundesley. 'We walked in a landscape entirely new to my eyes,' he recalled, 'flat and chequered, with all the trees slanting one way, their branches welded together in tortuous forms by the relentless winds.' It was after this visit that Nash painted *The Cliff to the North.*

In 1919 Pellew married the Slade-trained Emma Marie Tennent and rented The Pightle at Overstrand. Local landscapes were depicted in a range of media including wood engravings, in which delicate variations of tone and texture were produced from sometimes coarse cuts. One engraving, *From My Window,* recorded the view from the house, looking towards the railway line.

The Pellews then bought a triangular plot of land between Southrepps and Trunch, on which, with the aid of local builder, they designed and built their own house, also called The Pightle. Amid a wind-swept landscape of bent and stunted trees, and plough-teams working in small, hedge-divided fields, the couple created a sheltered garden, complete with a studio. Here they remained, for the most part contentedly isolated (between visits from friends such as John and Christine Nash). During the Second World War Pellew was arrested as a spy while awaiting a train at Gunton station: he had received a letter in German, and was held until his British status was established. Otherwise, life was simple – with electricity arriving as late as 1955. By then the local scenery was fast changing: branch rail lines were running down, the last horses were being replaced by tractors, stooks were giving way to spent bales, bull-dozers and sprays were laying an exposed landscape bare. Claughton Pellew must have mourned the transformation of the peaceful places he had loved.

Both he and his wife, though Roman Catholics, chose to be buried in the surviving calm of the churchyard at Gimingham – across the fields from Mundesley sanatorium.

Peter Greenham *The Shore at Mundesley,* oil.

PETER GREENHAM (b. London, 1909) knew the north Norfolk coast from childhood visits; later, he and his wife, the painter Jane Dowling, were to bring their own children here for holidays. Thus it may not be fanciful to imagine his thoughtful beachscapes as subtle blends of memory and discovery.

The English graduate attended London's Byam Shaw School of Art from 1936 to 1939, where he also taught after becoming a schoolmaster in Oxford. In 1954 he joined the staff at the Royal Academy Schools, and was appointed keeper a decade later. The early 1980s found him as a visiting teacher in the life-room of the Norwich School of Art.

Peter Greenham's brand of academic naturalism, through landscapes and portraits composed of 'a multitude of flickering touches of paint', stems from fine drawing and free technique. A fellow Royal Academician, Bernard Dunstan, commented that the artist's restrained palette has 'steadily lightened over the years (while retaining the essential play between cool and warm that is the basis of his colour) towards the iridescent blues and creams of his later beach panels'.

A century ago, north-east Norfolk's flooded mesh of medieval peat workings was a lost wilderness: the rivers Ant, Bure and Thurne fed clearwater lakes festooned with waterlilies where otters made slides in winter, harriers hunted, bitterns boomed and the yellow flash of swallowtail butterflies brightened the June air. Further south, below the immense and treacherous tidal pool of Breydon Water, the unpolluted Yare wound towards the Wensum, while the pristine Waveney snaked into Fritton Lake and on to Oulton Broad and Lowestoft. Broadland's scattered inhabitants scraped a living by culling nature's riches, as reed-cutters, eel-catchers, wildfowlers. But even then windmills were turning marshes into meadows, and meadows into arable fields. Wherries loaded with marl, coal, timber and grain worked the 150-mile network of inland waterways. And soon similar vessels were being offered for holiday hire – often complete with skipper, cook and piano. These were the graceful heralds of a future tourist invasion.

THE KINDRED marsh and riverscapes of Broadland and Holland provided countless subjects for **Robert Bagge Scott** (1849-1925), whom Alfred Munnings held to be the best Norfolk painter since John Sell Cotman.

Born in Norwich and educated mainly in France, he travelled the world with the Merchant Navy, filling his sketchbooks with details of sailing ships and exotic locations. But he disembarked, to train at the Royal Academy of Antwerp under Albert de Keyser, study the work of the Dutch masters (just as Crome had once absorbed the art of Hobbema) and explore France and the Low Countries. He emerged with some meticulous paintings of peasants, dykes, barges and windmills; and a Dutch wife.

Robert Bagge Scott *Wroxham Bridge*, 1988, oil on paper, 25 × 39cm (right).

Returning to his native city, Bagge Scott produced largely unpeopled landscapes, still indebted to the Dutch School. Fellow artists prized most highly his charcoal and pencil drawings, which were often preparatory studies for oils. He played a prominent part in local art life – he was president of the Norfolk and Norwich Art Circle from 1899 until his death – and exhibited at the Royal Academy.

His successor as Art Circle president, the watercolour landscapist Geoffrey Birkbeck wrote: 'There was never carelessness or lack of unity in his work. There was never any doubt about the direction of the wind in those wonderful skies he painted. There was perfect precision and drawing about his boats ... His observation was used to the full.'

Unspoilt and in parts seemingly uncharted, Broadland was an idyll for late Victorian painters who took the subjects as well as the techniques of the Norwich School as their chief inspiration. Most notably, two friends could often be seen on the Broads and rivers at this time, rowing a dinghy and trailing a Noah's Ark type of houseboat (formerly a primitive hotel for eel-catchers) in their wake. At a suitable spot they would tie up and record selected views in deft pencil or watercolour before casting off once more on a voyage that might last for weeks. The pair, **Charles Harmony Harrison** (1842-1902) and **Stephen John Batchelder** (1849-1932), are now recognised as the finest Norfolk watercolourists of their day.

Theirs was not a brazen talent; they had no desire to amaze with virtuoso displays of technique, nor did they care to adapt, distort or prettify nature to achieve artistic goals. Rather, they were content to evoke, with scrupulous care and control of perspective, Broadland's magical atmosphere. Harrison

Stephen John Batchelder (above) and Charles Harmony Harrison (far right).

C. H. Harrison *Rowboats on Broad,* **1891, watercolour.**

expressed both men's priorities when he declared that he 'loved Nature, and after Nature, Art'. Batchelder demonstrated the pair's precision by writing on the back of most of his pictures an exact description of the subject, below which he would head two columns: the left-hand division outlined the 'Idea', while to the right 'Execution' detailed the manner of its painting and the paints and colours used. Whether capturing the glory of early morning, with the water glistening in a golden haze, sunbeams skating across a wherry's bow at noon, an afternoon storm or the ruffling of rushes in an evening breeze, the skill of these kindred artists was to convey the moods and mystery of a wonderfully elemental world.

C. H. Harrison was born in a squalid and over-crowded Yarmouth alley known as Row 33. Natural history became his favourite subject at school, while sketches made during youthful trips to Bradwell, Burgh Castle and Caister displayed yearning affection as well as natural flair. As he had to help with the family income, he was apprenticed as a sign-writer in the Row 45 workshop of a Mr Platt where he developed his colour sense and learned a great deal about

mixing and applying paints. In his spare time he completed his education by reading, visiting exhibitions and studying the methods of Cotman and Crome. If art was an unlikely escape route for a working-class lad, the army was a well-trodden path to adventure. And in 1859 – seeming to despair of painting – Harrison joined the Yarmouth Artillery Volunteers and later the Rifle Volunteers.

In 1870, however, Harrison's artistic ambitions were revived when a relative employed on an East Indiaman gave him a box of watercolours which had been left behind by a lady passenger. He had found his medium. Now, with his land and seascapes rapidly attracting the attention of local art patrons and commissions resulting, the budding artist was persuaded to embark on a professional career. After the death of his first wife in 1877, he married again and then moved to London, hoping to perfect his painting and seek professional advice on the sale of his work. But in barely a year he returned: Harrison had hated the capital and had probably destroyed most of his work completed there. Henceforward he shunned the major London galleries. Norfolk formed his entire

focus and when, in 1880, a deep friendship developed with Stephen Batchelder (whom he had first met during an earlier sketching trip to Corton), the most productive phase of his life began.

S. J. Batchelder had worked in a Norwich photography business before transferring to a post in Yarmouth. Although he was to remain fascinated by the camera, he longed to express himself with pencil and brush. So he enrolled at the Yarmouth College of Art to study the underlying principles of drawing and painting. As a child in Lancashire (although of East Anglian stock) he had sketched incessantly – later decorating the scenery used by his showman father, who toured with a diorama in which he exhibited panoramas and dissolving views. But his training was disrupted by frequent travelling and, when the family returned to Norwich at the end of Batchelder's school years, he then had to set about making a living. Not until the age of 32 did he feel able, like his new friend Harrison, to support a growing household by painting. He bought a small boat named Smudge and launched himself as a recorder of Broadland. And, further echoing his artistic ally, Batchelder served with the Norfolk Rifle Volunteers where he too gained distinction as a marksman.

Watercolour suited the preference of both painters for speedy execution, and their need for prolific output. Harrison's biographers Arthur Patterson and A. H. Smith said of him: 'The rapidity with which he worked surprised many notable artists who accompanied him on his sketching tours. There was no restless choosing of positions, no laborious preliminaries characteristic of the plodder. He saw the picture at once, and in the rapid transference to paper, nothing was lost. His colouring was faithful, his knowledge of perspective complete, and a few strokes were sufficient to mark the details, which invariably distinguished his studio work.' Batchelder's records were rather more exhaustive. The hallmark of his finished work became the skillfully drawn wherry, most frequently depicted on the River Bure, while his friend delighted in a motif of reeds and waterlilies throwing shadows across translucent water.

After turning 50, Harrison began to ail with deafness, rheumatism and depression. A poor business sense and the burden of supporting 13 children had drained his energy and finances. Increasingly housebound, he was forced to turn out hundreds of small pictures for quick sale, and at times the famous care and honesty gave way to mere potboiling. He died defeated at 60, in an uncanny repetition of the demise of Cotman. A bunch of Norfolk reeds and rushes decorated his coffin. Batchelder worked on, until forced by failing eyesight to abandon painting at the age of 81. He died 18 months later at his home, 7 Garrison Road, Yarmouth.

S. J. Batchelder *Wherry on Breydon, Great Yarmouth Beyond,* **watercolour.**

ONE OF THE most prominent British Impressionists, **Henry Herbert La Thangue** (1859-1929), lived at Horsey from 1884 until 1891 after initially training in Paris. Here, he found the rural seclusion and patterns of country labour that he championed in his art.

H. H. La Thangue *Landscape Study*, 1889, oil on canvas, 51 × 61cm.

La Thangue, like his friend George Clausen, was influenced by the French painter Jules Bastien-Lepage, who had depicted the hard lives of poor people in the village of his birth. The Frenchman and his admirers painted scenes of social realism *en plein air* – out of doors, on the spot – with tonal harmonies created from a low-key range of colour. In Norfolk, with further inspiration from the Broadland photographs of Peter Henry Emerson, La Thangue put naturalistic theory into practice. Some of his pictures from this period also display traces of allegory and symbolism.

Although celebrating rural remoteness, La Thangue remained in close touch with events in the capital and on the Continent. He was instrumental in setting up the Francophile New English Art Club, but eventually resigned after the failure of his campaign for a national exhibition open to all artists. From the 1890s, after a move from Norfolk to Sussex, he showed ever stronger interest in light and colour – bolstered by frequent visits to Provence.

In 1914, Walter Sickert wrote: 'What makes La Thangue's work particularly interesting is that, while he is using the language of the day in painting, that is to say an opaque mosaic for recording objective sensations about visible nature, he is using it in a personal manner ... You cannot name any painter who is doing, better, what La Thangue is doing extraordinarily well.'

Of the next wave of Broadland artists, born in the 1860s, **William Edward Mayes** (1860-1952) was the most influenced by Batchelder and Harrison. The son of a Yarmouth sea captain, he inherited a life-long interest in boats, and was to be credited with the invention of a rowlock. After retiring as the manager of Yarmouth Foundry and moving to Palgrave Road, he had more time to devote to his watercolours of windmills, river scenes and views around Breydon and beyond; he was often to be found cycling out into the countryside to make notes and sketches for his faithful, competent pictures. Perhaps at times he came across another talented watercolourist, **William Leslie Rackham** (1869-1944), who lived at 82 Rosary Road, Norwich, for the last 46 years of his life but whose waking hours were claimed by Broadland. Poor Rackham. He was a clever colourist and had some success exhibiting his work locally; in 1927 he even published a book, *Everybody's Broadland*, which he had written and illustrated himself. But fortune eluded him. Many of his pictures were sold for a few shillings or exchanged, it is said, for glasses of beer. Slender means forced the purchase of cheap materials. Over time his beautiful blues, wrought in schoolboy paints, tended to turn to brown. Today some of this artist's finest work – if surviving at all – has faded into almost blank sheets of paper.

The 1880s gave birth to another brace of gifted watercolourists who were to be drawn to Broadland. **Charles A. Hannaford** (1887-1972) – son of the landscape painter Charles E. Hannaford, who studied under Stanhope Forbes, exhibited widely and lived in London and Norfolk – ran Broads Tours from Wroxham. Inspiration for his pictures (as well as his book *The Charm of the Norfolk Broads*) lay in all directions, and he often exhibited the resulting work with the Royal Society of British Artists. A still more substantial talent was **Charles Mayes Wigg** (1889-1969), who was born in Nottingham, painted during childhood visits to Florence and studied at the Norwich School of Art. He served in the First World War but was invalided out of the army after being injured at Gaza. For many years he produced his firmly drawn and powerfully coloured paintings (plus handsome etchings), in which wherries were usually predominant, from a studio in Brundall, where he lived with his parents. Later he found a place of his own at Barton Turf and, unable to drive a car, Wigg would travel from here on regular sketching trips by boat or bicycle. His career came to an abrupt end in 1952, when he married his mother's nurse: she prevented him from painting and even broke his brushes; together the couple burned piles of pictures. When finally a widower, Charles Wigg was unable to pick up where he had long before left off. He spent his last years with his brother in Eastbourne.

But the artist whose name may be most synonymous with Broadland is **Edward Seago** (1910-74), a portraitist and one of Britain's most popular landscape painters of this century. His annual post-war exhibitions in London, at Colnaghi's, were celebrated successes: long queues formed; numbered catalogues were issued limiting potential purchases to one; almost every show was sold out within an hour of opening. Although Seago was denied critical acclaim, his peers elected him a member of the Royal Society of British Artists in 1946 and of the Royal Society of Painters in Water-colours in 1959. And if his sweeping depictions of windy, wide-open expanses of Norfolk delight the eye, his private story fires the imagination.

Edward Brian Seago was born in Norwich, the son of a coal merchant. At the age of seven he developed a heart complaint, which confined him to bed for several years. The ailing child took to painting scenes from his window, but his burgeoning talent was discouraged by his parents who wanted him to pursue a business career. On recovering, he studied briefly at the Royal Drawing Society, winning a

A S A WILDLIFE HAVEN, Broadland has long attracted wildfowlers – and, of late, flocks of 'twitchers' who shoot only with cameras. For much of this century the area was also home to two migrant bird painters of great skill and sensitivity.

John Cyril Harrison (1898-1985) and **Roland Green** (1890-1972) were watercolour artists whose love of ornithology was matched by a feeling for Broadland scenery. They were experts in bird anatomy, Green being the son of a Kent taxidermist and past employee of London's Natural History Museum, Wiltshire-born J. C. Harrison having sketched and studied the subject during early years in British Columbia. Both saw service in the First World War before resuming their prime interest: Harrison then trained at the Slade (where Professor Tonks insisted that he should not paint until his draughtsmanship was secure). While both men enjoyed sketching trips to Scotland, and Harrison also worked as far afield as Iceland and South Africa, the Norfolk Broads – often viewed from a boat – provided their favourite habitat.

From his base at Hainford, Harrison worked on portraits of game birds, wildfowl and birds of prey, excelling especially in the depiction of frozen moments of flight. And at Hickling, where he was known as the 'hermit artist' – despite being a popular attraction at fêtes and festivals with his talent for drawing lightning sketches of birds to order – Roland Green blurred the barriers between the human and animal world. Here he lived firstly in a houseboat, using the tower of an old drainage mill as a studio and observation post, then he moved to a thatched, nest-like bungalow so close to the broad that it was a domain for ducks and frequently flooded. Water was his natural element. Only in his final years did he retreat to a drier residence in the village, while still returning to work on his delicate pictures in his old home among the reeds. Like J. C. Harrison, he knew every Broadland bird: he once painted a mural for his patron, Lord Desborough, which showed all the species to be found on the Hickling nature reserve. Both artists knew the precise changes of bird plumage wrought by age and season, and the sheen of a particular wing as it was struck by the light of a Norfolk sunset.

Roland Green *Wigeon Alighting – Hickling Broad*, watercolour, 24 × 19cm (below) and J. C. Harrison *Avocets*, watercolour (bottom).

Charles A. Hannaford *Windmill on the Norfolk Broads,* **water-colour, 24 × 37cm (above).**

THE ROMANTICALLY isolated ruins of the medieval St Benet's Abbey, situated next to a later and now sail-less windmill, have attracted many artists working in East Anglia. Here dilapidation combines with drama. Henry Bright painted the scene in a thunder storm; Edward Seago added a rainbow and brilliant light. In one of 16 coloured wood-cuts, illustrating Hayter Preston's book *Windmills* (1923), **Frank Brangwyn** (1867-1956) depicted St Benet's amid brooding blues and blacks.

Brangwyn was one of the most acclaimed artists of his day. After training as a draughtsman under William Morris, he lived in London and later Sussex, and travelled widely (the plates in *Windmills* were drawn from six countries). He produced fine drawings, etchings, lithographs and watercolours as well as vividly coloured oil compositions influenced by the grand manner of the Venetian decorators.

Frank Brangwyn *St Benet's Abbey,* 1923, watercolour, 41 × 30cm (right).

Elected a Royal Academician and knighted, Brangwyn was still at the peak of his fame when he made his wood-cut of St Benet's Abbey (an oil painting of the same subject is now in the Wolverhampton Art Gallery; there are also several watercolour studies). Two years later he was chosen to paint huge House of Lords murals commemorating the First World War. The work, which the artist considered his best, took seven years to complete but led to bitter wrangling, culminating in rejection. After such a blow, Brangwyn and his reputation sadly declined.

Edward Seago *On the Thurne, Norfolk,* oil on board, 56 × 91cm (above).

Edward Seago *Melting Snow, Ludham,* oil on board, 30 × 41cm (below).

special prize at the age of 14, and was instructed in landscape painting by Bertram Priestman: otherwise, the artist was self-taught. Reacting against the imprisonment of his childhood, the 20-year-old Seago joined Bevin's Travelling Show. Subsequent tours across Britain and the Continent were to provide the material for many pictures recalling the work of Alfred Munnings and Laura Knight, as well as two illustrated books chronicling circus life. Seago also collaborated on several volumes with the poet John Masefield. He saw war-time service with the Royal Engineers until invalided out in 1944, after which Field-Marshall Alexander invited him to record the Italian campaign.

Throughout his adult life Seago could count on friends in high places: in 1953 he became an official artist of the Coronation, in public recognition of a remarkable association with the royal family. He was a frequent visitor to Sandringham and, in 1956, he accompanied the Duke of Edinburgh on a world tour, exhibiting the resulting paintings at St James's Palace and leaving Prince Charles 'totally captivated by the unique way in which he could convey atmosphere on canvas and by the living texture of his

Edward Seago *A Norfolk Village,
Aldeby,* **oil on canvas,
76 × 101cm.**

pictures'. Although he journeyed all over the world – often sailing on his sea-going ketch Capricorn – in search of fresh compositions and colour contrasts, Seago was always elated on returning to what he called the 'cool greens and greys' of East Anglia and his home at The Dutch House, Ludham.

He was equally at ease in oils and watercolour, but over the years his method of painting changed. Having first drawn from life, he took to working up notes and sketches in the studio as he was anxious to capture atmosphere rather than pure topography. His many admirers marvelled at an ability to create a quick impression and the feel of a place with a minimum of brushstrokes; and he influenced many other East Anglian artists – including Norfolk's Ian Houston, whom he persuaded to switch from bird to landscape painting. Yet his critics sniffed that the work of a dazzling young talent had ceased to develop.

Never robust, Edward Seago was dogged by periods of disability throughout his life. But his final illness was brief: a brain tumour killed him at 63. His ashes were scattered over the Norfolk marshes he had loved so loyally.

Fred Taylor *Pull's Ferry and Cathedral, Norwich*, 1929 (above); Rowland Hilder *Pull's Ferry and Cathedral, Norwich*, 1940 (below); William Lee Hankey *The Flower Market*, 1935 (right). All three artists found success beyond the realms of the commercial poster. Rowland Hilder has shown the greatest allegiance to East Anglia, producing memorable images in pencil and watercolour from the King's Lynn Custom House to the Essex marshes.

Alfred Munnings, looking back in 1950, recalled the Norwich he had known in the 1890s as being largely unchanged from the days of Crome and Cotman. 'No wonder it had its famous Norwich School of Painters,' he wrote, 'for the artist is dependent on his environment, and no artist had a more truly picturesque home than this old city of gardens, with its cathedral, its fifty churches, its river with wherries, boats and barges, quays and bridges.' Waxing lyrical about a maze of alleyways, backstreets and courtyards unwinding within the city's medieval walls, he added: 'Such an unlimited wealth of motifs would tempt the dullest painter.'

On his first visit to Norwich, in 1918, when the city still extended barely a mile beyond its medieval boundaries, **Arthur Davies** (1893-1988) painted a watercolour of Sprowston Mill; 70 years later, he completed his final picture – of the street called Tombland. He filled the decades in between with thousands of graceful studies of his adopted county. Although he was born amid the mountains of rural Wales, Norfolk became his natural home. At the age of 94, a few weeks before his death, he recalled his earliest impressions: 'Here was such a fine old cathedral city; and you were so quickly in the country, where the subjects of the Norwich School rose up in front of you.' It was indeed as if his hero, John Sell Cotman, had packed his paints away and departed the scene mere moments before.

An only child, Arthur Davies had learned to love landscape during lonely wanderings beyond his parents' house in remotest Cardiganshire; and from such emotion came a desire to paint. Each summer he would fill water pots and clean brushes for two illustrators who took a cottage nearby. Arthur's family warned that art offered no financial security. But, won over by the boy's unswerving dedication, they determined that he should receive a proper training, which was to lead from Carmarthen to Dublin's Metropolitan School of Art. On the outbreak of the First World War, Arthur escaped active service, and probable death, due to a suspected heart defect. The apolitical art student was nearly a victim of the 1916 Easter Rising, however, when a sniper's bullet shattered a shop window as he passed. Eventually enlisting, he took up a clerical posting to Cambridge

Arthur Davies *Norwich Cathedral from Fishergate,* **oil on board, 30 × 41cm.**

and here, armed with his sketchbook, he sold drawings of the colleges for 10s and 6d each.

On a visit to a Norwich cousin, he was at once enraptured with what he saw. Wherries were arranged below Bishop's Bridge, and Mousehold Mill – which was to burn down a decade later – shone 'a glorious dove-grey in the sunlight'. Although he was establishing a reputation in Wales, where Augustus John awarded him first prize in a National Eisteddfod competition, he moved to Norwich permanently in 1923. He had a series of lodgings and studios in the city, before taking over his cousin's semi-detached house on Earlham Road, in the south of the city. Times were tough: for many years a good week would be one which brought in £4. Nevertheless, the artist was gaining recognition and exhibiting widely: the Royal Academy showed his work annually between 1936 and 1967; he was elected a member of the Royal Society of British Artists in 1939 and of the Royal Cambrian Academy three years later. But his

chief joys in life were a delight in the landscape, friends among fellow artists (Munnings was remembered showing undried canvases to his dealer) and a passion for paint. In 1988 he would still don a white coat each morning, and climb to his back bedroom studio to paint while the light was at its best – regretting only that he could no longer work nights.

He used oils, pastels and black and white, and produced competent portraits and often striking flower pieces: but his strength lay in watercolour land, sea and cityscapes of an unspoilt East Anglia. At first these works relied on their formal qualities, with skilled draughtsmanship most evident in topographical views. As time went on, however, the essence rather than the direct appearance of places he loved came to the fore; with a stroke of pale green shimmering on both a ship's stern and its watery reflection, or a dash of red glowing on a jacket, the artist would anchor a scene so delicate that it might otherwise drift away.

During the 70 years spent charting his adopted region, Arthur Davies saw bombs and bulldozers smash landscapes that had lain undisturbed for centuries. Towards the end, working from sketches that might be a day or six decades old, he was painting mostly the past. But he delighted in each fresh discovery of an undamaged and undrawn site, and he always looked forward: 'What's new in the world?'

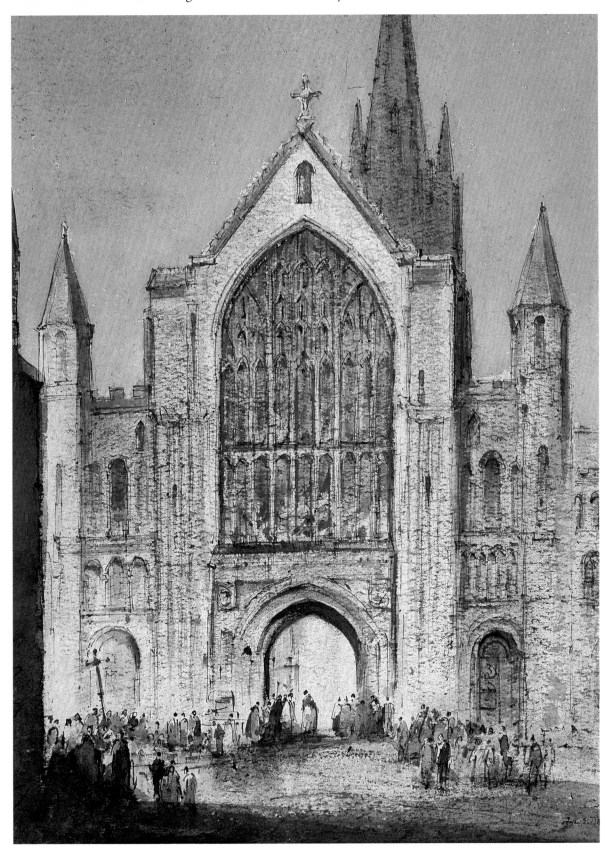

Arthur Davies *Norwich Cathedral in Floodlight*, 1951, watercolour, 42 × 30cm.

Arthur Davies – still working in his studio at the age of 90.

was his usual greeting, whenever friends called. Davies felt that to breathe a scene into life on paper required speed and spontaneity – once remarking of his rapidly-executed sketches, 'after half-an-hour you begin to fumble'. The Norwich painter Colin Self explained his fellow artist's appeal in the following way: 'His technique is nice. He would make a swift, impressionistic pencil sketch and then the colour would be put on to emphasise the life. It's like Constable's sky and cloud pictures, which capture the light and the breeze in that quick way. Light is so transient: you have to be quick as light to catch it.'

Against such nimbleness was matched a remarkable steadfastness and faith. For Colin Self, Arthur Davies was 'a true localist, with the kind of intelligence that preserves humility. How else could someone remain so modest, open, lively, energetic and full of almost a youthful passion and a love of his subject for so long? It is astonishingly rare. Picasso, who lived until he was 90, had this phase and that phase: he was one of my heroes, but Arthur Davies was too.'

In the early 1960s, when the Beatles were making revolutions in music, Pop Art saw a similar burst of iconoclastic energy. It featured Peter Blake, David Hockney – and **Colin Self** (b. 1941), who drew cinemas, sofas and women with fur coats, long gloves and bee-hived hair. Behind such metropolitan glamour there lurked a sense of time running out, of scandal, corruption and Cold War leading to Armageddon.

While Hockney left swinging London to become a celebrity in Los Angeles, Self returned to his regional roots. Twenty years later, in 1986, he was back in the capital with a vast and virtuoso show at the Institute of Contemporary Arts. The display, which its maker dubbed 'a jumble sale, a bomb of creativity splatting the walls, in a world of minimalist specialisation', was a triumphant return by a man whose art went far beyond the perceptions of pop. Often misunderstood, rejected and ignored – and, to protect his integrity, sometimes living below the poverty line – he had never stopped working as he wished. In his fertile creativity, a response to personal pressures was now mixed with an avowed ruralism and a cry for old Norfolk.

Colin Self, who was born near Rackheath, and who returned to live in nearby Thorpe, on the outskirts of Norwich, traces his Norfolk ancestry from the Domesday Book. He regards East Anglia, Holland and Friesland as 'one country separated by sea' and yearns for a shared golden age of rustic freedom. In Norwich School paintings he has a sense of 'Nature's bounty, of that boundless space created in the main by Mousehold Heath, which in those days stretched from Norwich Cathedral walls to South Walsham over ten miles away to the east. Forest overlooked Norwich on its eastern boundary beginning at Ketts Hill and Mussel Hill (now Gas Hill), oaks stretching for miles. The favourite place in all England for Romanies, according to George Borrow in his *Lavengro* and the place where the last true gypsy King and Queen were buried.' Self rages against the enclosure movement, with its legacy of dispossession, and sees that trend continuing today with booming property development in the countryside; he brands the forest of post-war housing estates 'Outer Bungolia'.

The son of a sign-writer, decorator, and maker of furniture and artefacts, Colin Self has inherited a craftsman's feel for a range of media. But manifold ideas and an unshakeable belief in his own meandering creativity have not always found favour. As a student at the Norwich School of Art, he says he was saved by the sympathy and support of Michael Andrews; when 'marked out for a failure' at the Slade, he was rescued by praise from Blake and Hockney, who visited, became his friends and bought his work. In this artist's makeup there is something of the Polish anarchist from whom he claims distant descent. He charts his own course. Scorning the fashions and commercial concerns of the art world, Self abandoned the drawings that had made his name. For a time he took up ceramics in Germany and later hid out in rural Scotland, where he slowly resumed sketching, also producing powerful watercolour landscapes. But it was in Norfolk, despite the break-up of his marriage, and conflicts with local officialdom, that a passionate inventiveness returned.

Grouped as 'Works of Fusion', Self's output since 1980 has covered collage, watercolour, oils, drawing, photography, sculpture and ceramics. Everyday objects, often collected from dumps (wrappers, matches, string: the detritus of a throwaway culture), spill over his 'people's art'. In *Ploughman,* corrugated cardboard evokes furrowed earth; elsewhere, a shoal of hair-clip fish swims towards capture in a hair-net, a brilliant sky emerges from $\frac{1}{2}$p stamps. As with Picasso, ideas explode like fireworks: but the materialism of society and the desolation of urban development are often central themes.

Most striking of all is a series of Norfolk landscape drawings – lyrical charcoal expressions of loss, with the paradoxical optimism that exact articulation brings. These gritty pictures are made with lumps of carbonised material, which the artist salvages from bonfires. He finds commercially produced tubular lengths of charcoal too fragile and 'phoney', whereas the irregular shapes of burnt wood once used by prehistoric cave and pottery painters are 'natural in spirit'. He enjoys employing a 'fundamental material in a computer age'.

The charcoal studies are autobiographical – what the artist calls 'self-portraits from the inside out'. The threnody for a landscape is also a song of lost innocence after the end of childhood, the death of friends and relatives, the sum of losses in a life. Thus a silo heap near Aylsham, depicted in *Passing Cloud,* resembles an ancient burial mound. In *There Are Places I Remember,* rooks swirl into a darkening sky as a ghostly light illuminates the chalked markings on an empty highway. Lines of communication are recurring motifs and metaphors in Self's work, as in *The Day My Auntie Eva Died – Double Crossing.* And co-existing in *The London Train (Late Night At Norwich (Thorpe) Station)* are the excitement of the rail centre and the trauma of urban development. This picture, moreover, was drawn hours after Self had decided to turn down an exhibition offer in the capital, and expresses both his pleasure at seeing the London train and relief at not being on it.

Most recently, the artist has been working on drawings of the Acle market and auction sale. This weekly event, which Self sees as a remnant of ancient Norfolk, is depicted with 'a roughness and a poetry like a naturally indigenous accent'. He longs to create a masterpiece about the crowds at Norfolk sales

Colin Self *Double Crossing (The Day My Auntie Eva Died),* **1985, charcoal and white chalk, 56 × 76cm.**

('I almost see Breughel's *Wedding Feast*'), and adds: 'When I draw I am not drawing the strict perspective view; it's more like somebody making up an essay from an environment.'

Another of the giants of post-war British art was born in Norwich and, like Colin Self, lives quietly in his native county. Exhibiting his paintings in public only rarely, he shows himself with great reluctance. Indeed, reported sightings, at points across north and central Norfolk, or in a village south of Norwich, where he is said to work all day and every day in a former chapel, are like glimpses of a bittern or corn-crake. **Michael Andrews** (b. 1928) is a reclusive painter of autobiographical pictures, sometimes in an East Anglian setting.

His first home was at 142 Glebe Road, Norwich; his father, a strict Methodist, was an insurance agent in the city. Fascinated by the works of the East Anglian masters in the Castle Museum, and especially those of Cotman and Crome, he won parental approval for his early determination to paint. Before leaving the City of Norwich School, Andrews attended part-time classes in oil painting at the Art School, given by Leslie Davenport, a fine depictor of buildings and demolition. Then, after military service, came training at the Slade under William Coldstream, whose stress on objective recording of observable forms proved at odds with the student's concern with human behaviour and psychology. Andrews nevertheless found swift acclaim, particularly

Colin Self *The Ploughman*, 1983, packaging cardboard with added oil paint and gold leaf, 76 × 56cm (opposite).

Colin Self *The London Train (Late Night at Norwich (Thorpe) Station)*, 1984, charcoal and pastel, 56 × 71cm (below).

among fellow painters. Apparently losing his crippling shyness, he enjoyed pubs and parties and the excitement of the capital; he also taught at various times at Chelsea, Norwich and the Slade. But by 1977, when he had relocated to rural Norfolk, the shutters of privacy had long been in place. And since then the artist has continued to work with slow deliberation and single-minded application on a wide range of ambitious pictures, drawn from notes, memory and imagination. Overall, he displays a mastery of mixed media – in drawings and watercolours used as prompts for bigger works, in the complex screening of photographs, in the stencillings, the sprayings and the fluent brushwork with which he articulates exactly what he wishes to say in the large-scale paintings.

The former Slade Professor, Lawrence Gowing, coined the term 'the School of London' for a group of generally figurative modern British painters headed by Francis Bacon. Those sharing a sense of 'abundant and engrossing material' included Peter Blake, Jeffery Camp, Lucian Freud, Patrick George, David Hockney and R. B. Kitaj. But 'A is for Andrews,' wrote Gowing in 1980, 'for whom paint does more things better than for almost anyone alive.' Like his heroes Bacon, Freud and Giacometti, Michael Andrews instils a sense of alienation and mortality into his images. His concern with states of mind has encouraged a liberal use of symbols in work connected by a confessional thread. Friends may be placed with great clarity in otherwise blurred and anonymous party crowds, and there is a recurrence of dislocated Norfolk motifs: an early beach scene, *August for the People*, was based on the impression of boyhood holidays in Sheringham – with an added bandstand to be found in Chapelfield Gardens, Norwich; one in a series of balloon

Michael Andrews *S.A.X. a.d. 832*, 1982, oil and acrylic on canvas, 150 × 150cm.

paintings – denoting the buoyant or deflationary shifts of the human ego – shows a soaring ball casting a shadow over sand and dune that hints at Winterton; painted shoals, sometimes threatened by pike, derived from fish seen at Geldeston, near Beccles.

At other times, Norfolk is overtly depicted in this artist's work. A huge and disquieting group portrait of his family was painted in the garden of his parents' home, in Park Lane, Norwich. And, more recently, there have been summer and winter landscapes around Saxlingham Nethergate which show a typically precise use of paint contrasting with an enigmatic viewpoint (an absence of people, save for a shadowy horse-rider, made all the more eerie by scattered signs of habitation: roads, telegraph poles, a telephone box and half-hidden houses). A shared title, *S.A.X. a.d. 832*, inspired by the inscription on a sign in the village, compounds the enigma and perhaps the sense of intrusion into a very private world.

South Norfolk's undramatic, domestic scenery also inspired the Royal Academician **Robert Buhler** (1916-89), who lived at Moat House, Hethel, near Wymondham, from 1964 until 1970. Earlier, he had rented cottages in Essex and Suffolk (notably Lower House Farm, by the River Stour at Stratford St Mary). Throughout these periods, the spirit of East Anglia was to be distilled and abstracted into paintings of controlled power.

Born in London of Swiss parents, Buhler studied in Zurich, Basle and, back in England, at the St Martin's School of Art. A scholarship to the Royal College of Art was soon given up in favour of a studio in Camden Town. He met the leading lights of the Euston Road School – William Coldstream, Victor

Michael Andrews *S.A.X. a.d. 832,* **1983, oil on canvas, 152 × 152cm.**

Pasmore, Claude Rogers – at his mother's Soho café and bookshop, and came to share their liking for uncluttered composition and restrained colour (also their reputation as teachers of distinction). He created well-received portraits and still lifes in pastel and oils, until a love of the East Anglian countryside urged a shift towards landscape.

His interest was in colour and pattern. Amid the intimate scenery of his adopted region, he savoured small-scale and apparently commonplace motifs: stripes of crops, hedges, the trees and water around Moat House. An obituarist noted that he had 'set himself always against the overtly picturesque, and would make a vibrantly luminous evocation of place out of a foreground cabbage-field leading to a simple silhouette of trees and perhaps a half-hidden roof'.

But the artist who had once dabbled with abstraction was never a copyist. 'Buhler's landscapes appear at first glance as straightforward representations', wrote critic and former Tate Gallery director John Rothenstein. 'Their realistic look is illusory, for they are based upon elaborate geometric designs and their apparent straightforwardness is testimony to the thought devoted to their composition.'

He painted his landscapes outdoors, until he found that his quest for selection and simplicity was best pursued from drawings and colour notes in his London studio. But, whether drawing on reminders of East Anglia, the Continent or elsewhere, he always conjured up a sense of quiet space rooted in the real world.

Robert Buhler
A Norfolk Farmhouse,
oil on canvas, 51 × 61cm.

Great Yarmouth, wedged between sandy beaches and the muddy estuary of the rivers Bure and Yare, has always earned its living from the sea. As a port, it was long a landing point for huge catches of mackerel and herring; its quays retain the colour of foreign flags and the aroma of far-off places. As a tourist resort, its cheerful down-to-earth character remains unassailably English, resisting both the elements and the rivalry of cheap package trips to the Mediterranean.

If Yarmouth's heyday as a centre for traditional family holidays occurred between the wars, with an echo lasting into the 1950s, the sense of summer fortnights spent beside a bracing North Sea was best captured in the canvases of that time by **Campbell Mellon** (1876-1955). His art was not the stuff of travel posters or glossy postcards and he felt no need to prettify his scenes; rather, he celebrated the teeming coastline between Yarmouth and Lowestoft as he saw it, and shared in the pleasure of humanity at play.

Archibald Campbell Mellon was born at Sandhurst, Berkshire, and at first showed little aptitude for painting. Only from 1903, when he moved to Nottingham to work as a travelling salesman for a provisions firm, did he begin to paint seriously in his spare time. Lessons were taken with several local artists, including Carl Brenner, the nephew of Royal Academician B. W. Leader. The few pictures to survive from this period display rather lifeless drawing and a muddy palette dominated by dark brown (save, perhaps, for some views of the River Trent, which hinted that the artist could be moved to greater heights by feeling for a particular place). Mellon's painting might have continued in this stolid manner had he not joined the Nottingham Society of Artists, whose president from 1912 until 1930 was Arnesby Brown. Mellon was almost certainly aware of the great man's style and skill, for his paintings suggest that he was soon attempting to emulate it.

By 1918 the 42-year-old commercial traveller had determined on an artist's life. Helped by his young wife's inheritance and retaining an interest in a Lowestoft grocery business, he moved to Gorleston,

Campbell Mellon *Gorleston Beach*, 1925, oil on canvas, 41 × 53cm.

to a house overlooking the harbour. Such a radical change of direction may have been prompted by the First World War, in which Mellon had seen active and gallant service, despite strong pacifist convictions: the experience for so gentle a person, who railed to the end of his days against acts of inhumanity, must have been especially searing. And it cannot have been coincidental that his new home on the Norfolk coast was but a few miles from Haddiscoe, where Arnesby Brown spent each summer. For the three years after his arrival Mellon became the master's only known student. The two painters, who were to die within weeks of one another, remained life-long friends.

The first of 50 Campbell Mellon pictures to be accepted by the Royal Academy was exhibited in

Campbell Mellon in his studio (left) and a detail from his painting *A July Morning*, 1950, oil on canvas, 51 × 61cm (below).

1924. Entitled *August Bank Holiday, Gorleston on Sea,* the oil view signalled the shape of things to come: a mass of mostly youthful figures, tiny but each one deftly defined, paddle and build sandcastles, picnic, sunbathe, ride donkeys or shelter in beach tents, against a backdrop of promenade, jetty or pier. The naturalistic scenes seem to exude a tang of salt and to carry cries of frolicking children into the surrounding air. They are rendered in the blue-grey tones favoured by Arnesby Brown, but Mellon also emphasised an individual brightness by painting directly into the sun. The play of light on sand and water fascinated him; and the best of his subjects are dominated by magnificent sun-shot skies. Often cumulus clouds blow across the panel or canvas, sometimes becoming thundery, to give an authentic feeling of weather on the turn. Mellon's children appear to be braving the elements; racing to the water's edge before sudden rain drives them from the beach, while the sense of a moment seized also underlines the brevity of summer holidays.

On many occasions the artist embarked on drawing trips inland, often accompanied by the Norwich watercolourist Arthur Davies. Resulting paintings of the marshes and meadows of East Anglia were wrought in a quiet key of green. But, frequently heavy and ponderous, these landscapes rarely attained the vigour of the beach studies. During the Second World War Mellon left the vulnerable Norfolk coast for the safety of the Wye Valley, all the while painting the rural landscapes around him; but he readily returned to Gorleston for the last decade of his life.

Although occasionally bitter that his work was not more appreciated in his adopted town, the painter was gratified by recognition among his peers. In 1927 he was a founder member and first chairman of the Great Yarmouth and Gorleston Art Society (now the Great Yarmouth and District Society of Artists). And national honours also followed: in 1938 he was elected a member of both the Royal Institute of Oil Painters and the Royal Society of British Artists. Mellon's admirers include the actors Beryl Reid – who purchased a seascape from his studio for £5, when playing in the 1950 summer show at Yarmouth's Wellington Pier – and John Mills, who grew up in nearby Belton, the son of a local schoolmaster. Writing in the catalogue for the painter's London memorial exhibition, at Walker's Gallery, Mills wrote, with fitting understatement, 'I have been collecting pictures by various painters through the last 15 years and I always find that a Mellon painting can do more than hold its own in quite distinguished company.'

Mellon may have been a landscape painter of limited range, but his finest pictures remain fresh and vital. His shy manner and restrained palette earned him – rather unfairly – the nickname of 'Melancholy

Rowland Fisher, photographed in his studio in 1949.

Mellon', but his pictures remain an endearing celebration of childhood and of pleasure snatched beneath an unpredictable East Anglian sky.

Mellon lived at 2, and latterly at 1, Upper Cliff Road, one of Gorleston's turn-of-the-century terraced streets laid out between the High Street and the descent towards the harbour. By some strange chance, on arrival he discovered that a near neighbour was also an artist with ambitions beyond the amateur. Indeed, the appearance of the newcomer, and his evident dedication to painting, may have encouraged **Rowland Fisher** (1885-1969) to devote more energy to what had previously been merely an enjoyable pastime. During the 1920s Fisher developed distinctive painterly skills, and laboured early efforts gave way to marine pictures of great fluency. The neighbours became friendly rivals.

Rowland Fisher was born in Gorleston, the son and grandson of master mariners. Growing up on Cliff Hill, he drew the ships he could see from his home and longed to follow in the wake of his seafaring family. But his father – also a Trinity House pilot, before an early death – had forbidden it. So the school-leaver was apprenticed to a Jewson timber firm in Southtown; here he stayed for half a century, until retiring as sawmill manager in 1950. A sketchbook was always kept close at hand, to be filled with rapidly executed drawings, displaying a growing delicacy of line, whenever opportunity arose. Fisher helped to found the Great Yarmouth and District Society of Artists, following Arnesby Brown as its president, and remained an amateur painter in name only.

Rowland Fisher *Drifters Leaving the Harbour,* **oil on canvas, 102 × 127cm.**

Number 3 Upper Cliff Road, where Fisher lived with his sister for many years, is a cut above its neighbours: early on a look-out tower had been added when the building was converted into a boarding house, and thus it gained a commanding view of the traffic in the harbour and beyond to the open sea. Here, the artist would sometimes sketch, but he was long obliged to have as his studio a dark ground-floor room at the back of the house – which may have sharpened his preference for working directly from nature. Only late in life, when his sister's death left him free to marry, was he able to move his workplace to the front of his home, to make the most of the available light and the view.

Rowland Fisher was astonishingly prolific – a fact that long served to depress the price of his pictures.

He worked in various media, including etching and watercolour, and was also a skillful modeller of ships. But he was at his best, and most confident, when tackling oil paintings, often of substantial sizes. Here he would employ the palette knife as well as the brush, which suited his vigorous style and his liking for thick layers of paint. He aimed to impart a sense of motion, telling one interviewer: 'If there is no movement there is no life in a picture. Gulls are always useful; they swoop into almost every sea scene.' Untaught, he at times showed weakness when depicting figures, but there was more than compensation in strong design and draughtsmanship, and an emphasis on light as well as line.

Most of all, Fisher's work was an honest record based on observation, knowledge of the way in which

Rowland Fisher *Harbour Mouth, Gorleston from the Artist's Lookout,* 1948, oil on board, 23 × 27cm.

ships, docks and quays operated, copious sketches, and notes from trawlermen friends on details of fishing practices at sea. Thus he charted the fortunes of the Yarmouth fleet as it changed from sail to diesel. The town credited with inventing the kipper, bloater and fish finger would still depend on a marine harvest long after the rows of fishermen's hovels, where nets had once been stretched across narrow streets to dry, were levelled. Fisher caught the prevailing atmosphere. No finer tribute was paid to the artist's skill than a critic's remark that his sea was wet and his boats floated in the water.

Rowland Fisher also painted street scenes, which tended to depict Yarmouth and Gorleston as wintry outposts shrouded in mist or lashed by storms. And, especially in later years, he sometimes travelled by taxi to sketch views of the Yare and Waveney valleys. More distant scenes resulted from visits to France, Holland and Italy; and Cornish holidays led to his membership of the St Ives Society of Artists. London also beckoned: there he was elected a member of the Royal Society of Marine Artists, winning its Watts Prize in 1949 for the best picture portraying men working at sea, and later of the Royal Institute of Oil

Painters. Most fittingly, perhaps, he is represented in the National Maritime Museum with a painting of a four-mast barque.

To turn away from Yarmouth, and skirt around the vast expanse of Breydon Water, to what remains of the marshy meadows between Halvergate and Haddiscoe, is to step into the landscape of **John Alfred Arnesby Brown** (1866-1955). Here is the network of dykes lined with poplar and pollard willows; the flat horizon pierced by an occasional church, mill or sail; and the banks of clouds billowing in a sky forming three-quarters of the scene that are the key ingredients of a master's art.

Fishermen and farm labourers are sometimes glimpsed in Arnesby Brown oils, but they remain subservient to their surroundings. More majestic by far are the cattle lumbering through verdant pasture and gathering in foreground groups. Here the ox is king of beasts, painted with a breeder's appreciation of weight and bulk, the equivalent of a horse to Alfred Munnings. But Brown regretted the acclaim his efforts earned. Anxious not to be stereotyped, he omitted cattle from later pictures. Thus the windy expanses of his landscapes became still more marked.

Born in Nottingham, this keen sportsman almost achieved fame as a goalkeeper. However, a soccer contract with Nottingham Forest was rejected in favour of a training in art. Arnesby Brown attended the Hertfordshire school of Hubert von Herkomer, a painter of eminent Victorians and family groups. Inevitably, the talented student, who had exhibited at the Royal Academy as early as 1890, dabbled with portraits at first, until finding his heart and his feet in depicting the English countryside.

Although he was to be placed in the grand tradition of English landscape painting – encompassing Richard Wilson, Gainsborough, Constable, Cotman, Crome and Turner – Arnesby Brown was clearly influenced by French trends. He admired the Barbizon painters Corot and Millet and adored the Impressionist use of bold brushwork and broken colour to evoke atmosphere and spontaneity. By the early 1890s English artists taking their cue from France were clustering in Cornwall – at St Ives, or around Stanhope Forbes at nearby Newlyn – and

Arnesby Brown joined them. At about this time a friend with a house at Geldeston, near Beccles, invited him on a Broadland sailing holiday. The enchanted visitor extended his stay by taking rooms at The White House, Haddiscoe, a small farm situated on high ground overlooking the Waveney Valley. Here he made sketches of a moon-rise over the marshes for what became his first East Anglian painting, *Herald of the Night*.

In 1896 Brown married the painter Mia Edwards, and the couple spent their first summers together working from a cottage at Ludham. However, although Arnesby Brown found inspiration all over Norfolk and Suffolk, he could never dislodge his initial delight with Haddiscoe. He tried to rent or buy The White House, but was unsuccessful until 1905. After that, summers were spent at Haddiscoe and winters, among friends such as the writer J. M. Barrie, in Chelsea. By 1915 the artist was well enough established in Norfolk to be congratulated by the Great Yarmouth Corporation on being made a Royal Academician.

Arnesby Brown *Cattle on the Marshes,* **oil on board, 16 × 23cm.**

Reserved and taciturn, but with the bearing of a country squire, Arnesby Brown was judged a good companion and universally liked. His art came to have many imitators, though his wife was not among them. Mia continued with wistful portraits of children which suggested to some the poignancy of a childless woman. After her death in 1931 her widower moved permanently to Norfolk and here, apart from painting tours of Scotland, Cumberland and Nottinghamshire, he spent his final years.

Arnesby Brown's lifelong concern was with the effects of light on landscape, which he studied by acute observation and by working in the open air. And it was said that nobody had ever painted skies and clouds like him. In one picture, the tones of white and brown cattle wading through greenery might be transmuted by a sunset glow to pink and cream, gold and purple. In another, golden light filtered through dykeside willows to dapple the flanks of a grazing herd and spangle the blue-shadowed haze at their feet. Each tone and colour value would be reconsidered at home in the evening, with displeasure prompting revision or even destruction. It was partly because of this rigorous self-criticism that the artist's final output was not vast.

Over time the large youthful pictures were scaled down, often being worked out on the backs of cigar boxes. Conversely, small brushstrokes and close attention to detail gave way to broad sweeps of paint. Although compositions were simplified, a strong sense of design remained: there was never a trace of self-indulgence or an arbitrary gesture; each touch of

Arnesby Brown *Haddiscoe Church, Norfolk,* **oil on panel, 22 × 27cm.**

Arnesby Brown *The Coming Day,*
oil on canvas, 121 × 177cm.

paint added to the precision of the overall image. From a painter of high summer alone, he became alive to the nature of each season, capturing the tension in a landscape where the weather could change at any moment. Arnesby Brown sought subtle harmonies of colour and tone from carefully selected pigments: silvery greys, lilacs, creams and blues would be linked by a lush green; all would be laid on the canvas with a swirl of the brush and a smear of the palette knife. Even late pictures dwelling on themes of twilight, and striking an elegiac note, were painted with verve.

Arnesby Brown's growing simplicity of subject reflected the nature of the wild and windswept marshes at Haddiscoe, whose chief landmark, the round Saxon tower of the village church, became to him what Dedham tower had been to Constable: again and again it was worked into his design. Over time, the process of paring down the details of nature was also hastened by failing eyesight. For the last decade of his life the artist was virtually blind.

He found fame – exhibiting 139 pictures at the Royal Academy – but refused to have anything to do with dealers. Neither would he seek the help of anyone to make him a fashionable painter: the artist simply worked as he wished. Yet he gained admirers all over the world, and many made the difficult journey by road or rail to look over his studio, which stood in an old barn beside his cherished home.

In 1935 Arnesby Brown became president of the Great Yarmouth and District Society of Artists. Three years later, as his sight began to dim, he received a knighthood for his services to the nation's art. When unable to paint, he continued to be cared for by a housekeeper, kept up with cricket and football reports on the radio, still attended church each Sunday and held in his mind's eye the view over the marshes to the Waveney Valley. One frequent visitor was his parish priest, the Reverend A. R. Batchelor Wylam, who later wrote: 'A little lonely he could not fail to be, but he knew no bitterness and resentment in his enforced retirement. He would have liked to handle watercolour then, but he knew he had done good work, and that it would last.'

After the artist's death at the age of 89, an electric heating system and Bible were provided in his memory for Haddiscoe Church, where Mia was already commemorated by a stained glass window. Constable once wrote from London: 'I shall return to Bergholt, where I shall endeavour to get a pure and unaffected manner of representing the scenes that may employ me . . . There is room enough for a natural painter . . . Fashion always had and will have its day, but truth in all things only will last, and can only have just claims on posterity.' So it was and will be with Arnesby Brown.

Arnesby Brown *Full Summer,* **oil on canvas, 113 × 112cm.**

Mary Newcomb *Four Guinea Fowl*, 1985, oil on board, 91 × 61cm.

If surviving only in odd glimpses these days, there remains something fresh and tranquil about the sheltered landscapes in and around the Waveney Valley. Here persist some fine subjects for pastoral painters. A certain new-minted quality about the area's fields and willowed watermeadows has struck a deep chord with an artist named **Mary Newcomb** (b. 1922), who has never lost the child's ability to wake each morning and find the world astonishing. In endlessly noticing fresh details of nature and small incidents of rural life, this quiet, reflective painter draws inspirational delight.

By bicycle, bus, boat and train, or otherwise on foot, the intrepid non-motorist has explored the countryside – especially the lanes and tracks that criss-cross the Waveney Valley and extend into south Norfolk and north Suffolk. Here, since 1950, she and her husband have lived in a succession of ancient farmhouses (at Needham, Linstead Magna and Newton Flotman) amid children and assorted animals. No trip is too tortuous, for the artist is gathering glimpses of wildlife, farming activities and country ceremonies. From such raw material, a world is recreated where time is marked only by the seasonal clock, and no developer treads.

'Many of my paintings are of country events, fetes and festivals, markets or workers in the field', Mary Newcomb explains. 'Some are the results of an exchange of words with the occupants of a landscape. From the top of a bus going to town, I see a fox. I say "Fox, fox, the day is coming" – or to a boat from a bank the message goes out "Ferry me across the rippling water!"' Communion with a winter field inspires the phrase 'Think of me hopping bird and stone', while 'Bees are heavy and life is short' emerges from an autumn bank bristling with late flowers. Such lyrical titles prompt poetic paintings.

Equally, the artist can be attracted to the heavens or moved to record domestic detail: a butterfly stepping stiffly across the kitchen floor, drops of dew on some garden fronds, or the bickering of ducks whose friends have been carried off by a vixen. At times she hints at extraordinary links within the natural world, as when, in her painting *Too Much These Dandelion Heads,* a star-speckled sky finds an echo in luminous dandelion flowers soaring above the dark earth. Or she may suggest what happens in a landscape when we have left it (*After The Train had Gone* becomes three watercolour ponies at full gallop). Such thoughtful studies were appreciated by Ben Nicholson, who wrote to the art dealer Andreas Kalman: 'What appeals to me among other points is that so many . . . are imaginative ideas and not pictures.'

Pencil notes and drawings, like pages from a diary or travelogue, are stored in the artist's studio under headings such as 'Strange Situations', 'Things Bright in the Sky' and 'Bizarre and Jazzy Days'. Pinned to the window frame or lying in little heaps are fragments of colour: cards, posters, wrapping paper. And leaning against the walls are hardboard sheets and canvases – each mottled with pigment, each with its own assemblage of rainbow scraps and sketches. Plain white surfaces have no place here. 'I cover them with colour, then paint over that', Mary Newcomb confirms. 'Sometimes the picture will obliterate the first shades; sometimes, as I paint, the colour will blend beautifully with the background, so it remains.'

Working on perhaps dozens of pictures at any one time, she waits patiently until an emerging backdrop suggests a remembered or imagined moment. Layers of sombre-hued and richly-polished oil paint may underline an air of mysticism and mystery. Other paintings, more brightly coloured and lightly textured – and often with a gentle wit – have delicately stained backgrounds in pastel shades. There are also hybrids, where changes of heart are worked in to full advantage and freely admitted by their maker who says simply: 'On some of my finished pictures you can see where I have started on one idea and then painted another on top.'

The apparently artless Mary Newcomb, who was born at Harrow-on-the-Hill and had no formal tuition as a painter, has been labelled a naive, a primitive – or even a rural L. S. Lowry. But the ways in which she carefully restricts and simplifies, and

distorts the relationships between living forms, are anything but unsophisticated. As the critic Marina Vaizey has noted, her picture plane is deliberately flattened: distance and perspective are thrown to the winds; people may be dwarfed by plants, a chapel and wedding party lost in a field of sweet corn. But although size and scale run riot, the artist is, at the deepest level, faithful to nature – as befits a former teacher of the natural sciences. She says: 'My paintings are based on observation, but my training in zoology and botany makes me conscious that what I am putting down must be accurate – because what you see is not always what the facts are about the structure of things. My pictures come from the tension, the struggle, between the two.'

This highly feminine art is saved from whimsy by its creator's absolute sincerity and lack of self-consciousness. Specific subjects may be up in the clouds and beyond or down to earth among the patterning of woodlice beneath a log; but the idiosyncratic view remains intensely felt. Such sensitivity only adds to the charm of a painter who always understates, never insists.

The artist continues to work on ever larger canvases, but she remains a sublime observer of the minor event, however magnified. Thus she holds true

Mary Newcomb *Rider on the Shingle*, 1987, oil on board, 41 × 56cm (below) and the artist in her garden (above).

to the haunting emptiness of her beloved East Anglia, where age-old open spaces and a scarcity of dramatic features have been further stressed by modern land-scape management: hedges are now sparsely spread and wildflowers confined chiefly to verges beyond the sprayer's reach.

Mary Newcomb's greatest gift may lie in point-ing out surviving traces of an unspoilt world. A fellow spirit with the 'peasant' poet, John Clare, she presents us with tiny treasures of nature that pre-viously passed unseen in front of our blurred eyes or beneath our clumsy feet.

Whereas Mary Newcomb travels widely to record the patches of colour and random incidents which prompt her paintings, Waveney ruralist **John Morley** (b. 1942) has created an oasis of endless inspi-ration in his own backyard. 'Gardens', he has written, 'are magical places. The Persian word for garden is paradise. The walled garden for me is a private world, secure in a kind of timeless enchantment. My garden,

Mary Newcomb *Many Bees at Work Inside*, 1984, oil on canvas, 102 × 96cm.

where some imperishable drama has been perpetually and quietly enacted, is an imagined but real dream; a collection of ideas which haunt me, formally and pre-cisely arranged. There are no figures, only a magpie, flowers and trees. It is a personal statement about a very personal myth.' As he speaks of his plants, he is also speaking of his paintings.

This artist's retreat lies a mile or two from the isolated hamlet of Stoven, five miles from Beccles, by an ancient common that is approached along a single track. In accordance with East Anglian custom, North Green may formerly have been a place to which upright villagers banished the unwanted, such as unmarried mothers and simpletons. Where once there was a ring of dwellings, now only two remain. The house belonging to John Morley and his wife, the painter Diana Howard, retains a primeval sense of enclosure: a safe haven behind a palisade of walls and hedges. As the surrounding natural landmarks – the trees and ponds and hedgerows – have been filled and felled, the house and garden have become a new sort of refuge, almost an ark.

John Morley struck up a late friendship with Cedric Morris that was based more on a mutual love of gardening than of painting. Hundreds of roots and cuttings were exchanged and, when Morris died, Morley was allowed to transplant some of the master's famous irises and fritillaries. Now the North Green garden – with 300 varieties of snowdrop alone – is itself a noted work of art, attracting a stream of visitors. The plantsman has an ambivalent attitude towards his green passion, however, arguing that Morris, John Aldridge and John Nash all recognised that they would have been better painters had they not been such obsessive gardeners. Perhaps so. Yet, in each case, an affinity with growing things and an expertise in botany also helped to germinate pictures of rare accuracy and sympathy.

Raised partly on an estate in Kent, where his grandfather was a gardener, John Morley imbues his art with the earliest memories of childhood. The terracotta pots of auriculas, which have become his favourite motif, the apple trees and the baskets of redcurrants or quinces stem from a flourishing and well-ordered world, recalling the security of infancy. Although there is a settled and timeless air, the grainy light – and the inclusion of antique or Art Deco material and vases – may deepen an impression of nostalgia.

At Beckenham School of Art he studied along-side David Inshaw (who was later appointed fellow commoner in creative art at Trinity College, Cam-bridge) and both men subsequently became involved with the Brotherhood of Ruralists – a cluster of friends centred around Peter Blake. The group's art combined acute observation and imagination, cherished the countryside and revered such diverse influences as the medieval painters of illuminated manuscripts, Samuel Palmer, William Blake, the Pre-Raphaelites and Stanley Spencer. But whereas the rest of the Brotherhood looked to the West Country, John Morley and Diana Howard chose East Anglia, as the closest, cheapest unspoilt region to London. They were not entirely isolated, however, for established artists Peter Greenham and Allan Gwynne-Jones, (a Royal Academician and Slade teacher, who had visited Southwold as a child and later maintained a house at Wenhaston) were on hand to confirm that academic figurative painting still offered a powerful contemporary vehicle for a poetic personal vision.

In his painstakingly produced oils and water-colours, John Morley is preoccupied with perspective. In one early and ambitious garden picture, incorporating myth and mystery, and inspired by the line from an Elizabethan sonnet 'His helmet now shall make a hive for bees', he made a detailed model so that he had a physical reality from which to work. On other occasions he simulated moonlight with the aid of candles and evoked a cloud-streaked sky by studying milky tea left overnight in a saucer.

John Morley *Near the Pond, North Green*, **1983, watercolour,** **37 × 38cm (above) and** *North Green Farm in Winter*, **1982, oil on board, 23 × 28cm (left).**

For more complex and demanding works, such as *A Summer Garden*, the artist calculated the various vanishing points and falls of shadow by employing a wooden framework and strings. And even if the overall composition is imagined, the elements of each scene are drawn from careful observation.

Although he often paints landscape when on holiday abroad – with a particular fondness for the Alpine scenery that contrasts so sharply with East Anglia – at home he has recorded chiefly the view from his studio window, but many times over so as to capture the endlessly changing effects of light and season. Since his favourite barn was demolished, however, along with a fifteenth-century farmhouse whose

Prunella Clough *Closed Beach*, **1945, oil on canvas, 56 × 41cm.**

moulded ceiling had enchanted the architectural historian Nikolaus Pevsner, John Morley has turned still more firmly to the world within the walls of his house (a magpie's nest of collected objects) and the boundaries of his garden. His natural habitat remains supremely private, unruffled, unruined.

In restoring his house, which began as four near-derelict cottages, and tending a profusion of rare plants, the artist also gives shape to his creative impulse. The film-maker John Read says: 'It's as if he were seeking some authority or justification for his vision by constructing a corresponding reality in bricks and mortar.' Here he belongs, gathers moss, becomes ever more rooted. But John Morley does not completely raise the drawbridge on the outside world. He wages conservationist battles and dreams of buying a strip of land around his secret garden 'just to put the trees back'.

The sheltered nature of the Waveney Valley contrasts sharply with the nearby fishing port of Lowestoft. Positioned on England's most easterly point, the town sometimes seems crouched against gales and currents sweeping down from the Arctic. In summer it usually manages to throw off its wintry austerity like mourning cloth. But 1945 was an exception. Then, around Lowestoft – as elsewhere along the East Coast, the atmosphere seemed a far cry from the pre-war era of sandcastles and piershows. Large tracts of shoreline were still mined, tank-trapped and barb-wired against an invasion from Hitler that never came. In an oil painting entitled *Closed Beach*, **Prunella Clough** (b. 1919) depicted a stretch of sand occupied by blocks of metal and concrete, and spikes like starfish. Its mood conveys the sense of menace and desolation that marred the peace in an atom-splitting age.

A Londoner, Prunella Clough had known the north Suffolk coast from childhood, and between the years 1945 and 1951 she returned to construct a series of coastal compositions. Her *Dead Bird* was a bleak beachcomber's still life of a gull carcass laid out on a breakwater; and in *The White Root*, a smoothed and salt-bleached tree root – of the sort often uncovered by the tide at Covehithe – was set against splintery planking. These pictures present a vertical pattern of contrasting textures in an austere world of white, grey and black. Prunella Clough's studies in sculpture and graphics, at the Chelsea School of Art, were interrupted by the war, and a switch to patriotic work – mostly making engineering drawings. From these precise and rigorous labours she had emerged as a fully-fledged artist with a very personal view. But the combination of rich paint surfaces and a severe vision invited comparison with her friends in the Neo-Romantic movement – Robert Colquhoun, Robert MacBryde, John Minton and, later, Keith Vaughan.

Before it was fenced off to the public, Lowestoft harbour attracted crowds of townspeople and tourists, who would watch the trawlermen unloading and weighing their then-impressive catches. Prunella Clough loved the bustle of the place. Sauntering, sketching and taking photographs, she was often accompanied by David Carr, a painter who produced stark and Colquhoun-influenced pictures of working people, co-founded the Norfolk Contemporary Art Society and played host to visiting artists such as L. S. Lowry, at Starston Hall, near Harleston. In *Fishermen in a Boat* and *Lowestoft Harbour*, Clough used semi-Cubist arrangements of interlocking shapes to capture the quick and crowded atmosphere of a busy harbour, where the North Sea's booty was handled amid a clutter of masts, baskets and ropes. Here her

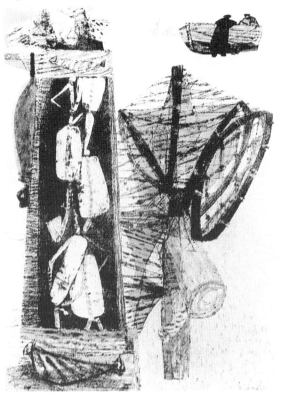

Prunella Clough *Eel Net*, 1948, coloured lithograph, 37 × 25cm.

Prunella Clough *Lowestoft Harbour*, 1951, oil, 163 × 107cm (left).

sombre palette was extended into murky greens and browns. Further along the coast – perhaps at Pakefield or Kessingland – the artist depicted dark Suffolk figures gutting skate or hauling in gleaming sprats. And, in what now seems a transitional work, she made a lithograph whose foreground was dominated by the intricate cork and mesh of an eel net, with two fishermen leaning into a boat relegated into the far distance.

After turning away from East Anglia, Prunella Clough found her subjects in the fabric of industrial life, literally in the nuts and bolts of modern urban society. From man-holes, gasworks and slagheaps, she distilled increasingly pure abstract paintings. But her work would retain the hard-headed poetry of something culled from the real world.

Lowestoft, the home town of Benjamin Britten, and focus for some of Prunella Clough's most distinctive paintings, also nurtured the artist **Jeffery Camp** (b. 1923). His early pictures were of figures on the pier, in the sea, or walking on the beach at Pakefield – braving the waves or buffeted by a bracing summer breeze.

Born at Oulton Broad, the only son of a cabinet maker and antique dealer, Camp began studying at the Lowestoft School of Art at 15; then graduated to Ipswich and Edinburgh. At the end of 1944, a travelling scholarship took him back to a Suffolk still affected by war. 'My parents had been evacuated to Eye,' he has recalled, 'deep in luscious countryside, where I fell in love with trees. I painted them through the seasons as they turned from green to yellow. Since I was painting the landscape, I was eligible for a bursary awarded to landscape painters which required that I go to London to show my work to Sir Alfred Munnings, then president of the Royal Academy. "What's all this bottle green?" he said. "Why don't you get out into the country and draw the thorn bushes?" Munnings showed me around the Academy throwing open doors as if he owned the place. But I had more modern ideas, and was thinking about Bonnard and Matisse, so was out of sympathy with him, though I did get the award.' An exhibition of Camp's resulting Suffolk landscapes was shown in Lowestoft in 1947 and many years later he was elected a Royal Academician.

From 1954, shortly before winning a commission to paint an altarpiece for the church of St Albans, Norwich, the artist began to work on studies of figures on or around the beach, always in motion. 'I like people in movement', he has said. 'I like the flux. Happiness is often to do with vitality. The activity of birds and sky and sea is somehow joyous, and helps towards happiness.' His early figures also look touchingly fragile against the sweeping force of the elements.

Although Jeffery Camp was soon to leave the Suffolk coast, with a national reputation assured through three shows at London's Beaux Arts Gallery, water remained crucial to his art. Based at Hastings, and married to the artist Laetitia Yhap, he painted the Channel and Beachy Head. Later, after moving to London, where he taught for many years at the Slade, Camp evoked the Thames. Holidays were working trips to Venice. A warmer, more lyrical, erotic and dream-like note began to spread through his work, until he was depicting entwined couples in rainbow colours, oblivious of the sea or river flowing past their locked limbs. It was a long way – but with an unbroken link – from windswept Lowestoft.

Jeffery Camp *Ravine, Pakefield,* **1954, oil on board, 41 × 41cm.**

Stanley Spencer (1891–1959) had a peculiarly powerful feeling for place. Most of his life was spent in a Berkshire village, which he glorified in scores of pictures. Much of his work combined the mundane with the miraculous – his neighbours were shown going about their daily tasks or listening to Christ preach at the Cookham regatta. But the artist also had a love of pure landscape. During key, though brief, periods in north Suffolk, he was moved to paint the wide horizon and haunting emptiness of the Wangford marshes, as well as a comic study of a crowded Southwold beach.

The link with East Anglia was provided by his first wife, **Hilda Carline** (1889–1950), who came from a family of gifted painters. Like Stanley and his brother Gilbert, she had trained at the Slade, at which time the younger sibling had been her suitor. Then, towards the end of the First World War, Hilda became a land girl on a farm near Wangford, where she also painted. Stanley, now pressing his own claim for her affections, thought one picture of sheep 'heavenly'. He himself had served in the war as a

hospital orderly and later as a soldier in the Macedonian campaign. The experience had shattered his peace of mind, while broadening his artistic outlook. In 1922 he joined members of the Carline family on a painting trip to the Balkans, and followed Hilda to Wangford in the autumn of 1924.

At Wangford, Stanley painted a panorama of the marsh beyond the village. It was his largest and most sophisticated picture to that date, and the unusual elongated shape set the pattern for several future studies. In a notebook entry written in 1937, he looked back on the effort as 'the first landscape I ever enjoyed painting. I very much liked the place. It was a wandering marsh land but full of character.' He also recalled that the vegetation, painted with typically painstaking detail, had hidden a 'lot of snipe making their funny noises with their wings'.

The courtship of Hilda was broken off several times, with Stanley blowing hot and cold towards the idea of a life-long commitment. But in March 1925 they were back in Wangford, to be married in a place where Hilda had been happy. After their wedding the

Stanley Spencer *Southwold*, 1937, **oil on canvas, 51 × 81cm.**

couple stayed on for a honeymoon – soon to be joined by Gilbert, at Hilda's request. Gilbert has recorded that the trio stayed in a cowman's cottage and painted out of doors – the new Mrs Spencer working on a 'long landscape'. Both brothers tackled views showing the local windmill (now gone) but Stanley was displeased with his picture, later confessing that he 'did not know how to do the road in the foreground'.

During this visit, Stanley also produced a small grey painting called *Sky at Wangford* and a larger work entitled *The Red House, Wangford,* which gave him particular pleasure. 'I enjoyed doing this', he recalled in 1937. 'The garden in front of the cottage was below the level of the road and well worn with little paths and the poor children were playing football there most days. I was a little puzzled at hearing the word "anguish" now and then uttered by one or other of them but it referred to the old oil merchant who came every Saturday afternoon and sold sweets as well as oil, hence his popularity.'

The artists also made several trips to Southwold: Stanley was invited to paint Lucy Silcox, headmistress of St Felix School, and both Hilda and Gilbert joined him in the task (previously all three had been engaged on portraits of each other). But the project was never

Stanley Spencer *Portrait*, 1934, **oil on canvas, 40 × 55cm (above).**

Stanley Spencer *The Month of August: On the Beach,* c. 1927, **21 × 35cm (below).**

completed. The patience of Miss Silcox, worn by protracted sittings, snapped when Stanley scrubbed his canvas almost clean.

Hilda and Stanley returned to Wangford the following summer, lodging with the Lambert family. Among several pictures completed during this visit, Stanley painted a landscape looking over a patch of nettles to the parish church where he had been married. It also seems likely that a pen and ink study *The Month of August: On the Beach*, drawn for the Chatto and Windus Almanac, derived from an outing to Southwold. The two figures in the deck chairs on the left of the picture are almost certainly the artist and his wife.

Stanley Spencer's trips to Suffolk in the 1920s were breaks from two huge projects which together dominated his working life for a decade. Murals based on his war-time experiences, commissioned for a memorial chapel in the Hampshire village of Burghclere, and a resurrection picture showing the inhabitants of Cookham churchyard returning to life, may be his masterpieces. They certainly left him drained of well-digested ideas, though his energy remained relentless. In Stanley's imaginative and

Stanley Spencer *Marsh Scene*, **oil on canvas, 35 × 46cm.**

THE YOUNGEST of nine children, **Gilbert Spencer** (1892-1979) was propelled towards painting by the urgings of brother 'Stan'. His work – skilful, sincere and direct – has lacked the public acclaim bestowed on his knighted brother, but both became Royal Academicians.

Although 'Gil' tackled Biblical themes and portraits, the bulk of his work stemmed from a warm response to the farms, fields and labourers of the English countryside. His crisply designed and coloured landscapes were generally completed in front of the subject. Berkshire, Dorset and Oxfordshire were favourite stamping grounds, between periods as a noted teacher in London and Glasgow. In East Anglia, he lectured at the Flatford Mill Field Studies Centre; also staying at Lawford Hall, near Manningtree, and with John and Christine Nash at Wormingford. Despite First World War horrors seen at Salonika, and the undoubted strain of being in Stanley's shadow, his pictures and personality never lost an air of optimism and Spenceresque mischief.

In 1970 Gilbert moved to north Suffolk, to a cottage at Walsham le Willows where he had visited the Martineau family (friends and patrons of both the Spencer brothers) regularly from 1958. Here he painted a few studies around Brook Farm and completed his autobiography. He died in a nursing home near Chelmsford in 1979.

While happy to retire to a corner of East Anglia which he found full of character, despite many changes, Gilbert Spencer was at best a reluctant recorder of the local landscape. 'As a painter,' he wrote, 'I do not care for Suffolk – it is too flat, and the farms of today with their cold steel sheds and cows, all of the same colour, each with a bedside light at night, and *The Times* provided with their breakfast, would have killed my farm pictures stone dead.'

Gilbert Spencer *Self Portrait*, **aged 18, oil on canvas, 51 × 32cm.**

Stanley Spencer *Marsh Scene, Wangford,* **oil on canvas, 43 × 129cm (above).**

visionary works the use of distortion now became more dramatic, and his patterning verged on the overpowering. In his overriding aim to stress the holiness of all creation, he risked a straining for effect. At the same time the artist was beset by personal turmoil as a far from easy relationship with Hilda was threatened by his infatuation with Patricia Preece. For a time he hoped that they might share their lives in a union free from conventional constraint. However, 1937 saw him reluctantly divorced from Hilda then wed to Patricia in May – a marriage effectively ended by a disastrous honeymoon. Stanley remained obsessed with Hilda for the rest of his life; he continued to visit her after her breakdown and confinement in hospital in the 1940s and wrote her hundreds of letters, many after her death in 1950.

In the summer of 1937, Stanley – already estranged from Patricia – still plotted for Hilda's return. He was convinced that if only they could get back to Suffolk, to the very bedroom of their honeymoon, to the beach at Southwold where they had searched for cornelians, all would be well again. Hilda regarded his pleadings as adulterous. Stanley left for Wangford alone and, once installed with the Lamberts, he revisited old haunts. 'I walked to the spots from whence 11 years before I had painted landscapes', he wrote in 1938. 'I got through the fence and walked over the marshland to where there used to be a clump of stinging nettles which in 1926 I had painted . . . and they were still there. I felt like a ghost.' He was relieved to find that the surrounding scenes displayed the 'mystery' and the 'special effects' he had captured in his pictures of them.

The morning after his arrival in Suffolk, the artist began a major oil painting of Southwold beach. He found the 'dirty washing water colour' sea was

'splashed by homely aunties' legs and the air was full of suburban seaside abandonment'. Each day he regained his vantage point between two beach huts by remembering the distance between two piles of dog dirt. He watched the holidaymakers – a girl writing a letter, sunbathers, a group of young people 'swaying about and singing badly' – with an interested but distant eye. 'I felt a kindred feeling with the bathing suits on the line in front of me,' Stanley confided to his notebook, 'in the sense that they seemed to be taking no part as I was not with the activities on the beach.' The enamel-like surface of the finished picture – resulting from the typical Spenceresque use of a single layer of pigment, with each interlocking detail painted separately – brilliantly captures the feeling of summer holidays by the sea. He wrote: 'There are about fifty repetitions of this same view. Another view which would have been interesting was standing on a fallen pile on the beach and looking along the beach at the succession of partitioned worlds of seaside and seasiders divided by loose hanging awning which I presume is a wind screen. One is seen in this landscape edge on.'

The private crisis of the 1930s also left the artist with perilous finances. He hated the speed with which he had to work to earn his living, and could be disdainful about the saleable scenes he was forced to produce. 'My landscapes compared with my other work are carried out with a hard relentless persistence and dogged determination to go through with it, which gives them a competent and finished but lifeless and hard look', he wrote around this time. 'They lack the informing ingredients of my own great liking and desire and they are metallic and empty as a result. They are shells and cases with no contents.' Stanley's tenacity was beyond doubt. During the 1937 visit to Suffolk he painted another landscape, which became *The Cottage at Wangford.* After working from the same spot for 11 successive afternoons, his easel balanced on a well, he felt that he had been rooted there for a lifetime. Later he was to tell Hilda that he 'hated doing landscapes' and did them 'solely for money'. For him, 'place-feeling' was something different. 'The only really significant love affairs I have ever had have been with places, rather than with human beings', he once wrote.

On the lonely marsh at Wangford, Stanley Spencer appears to have felt an affection of such intensity that it illuminated an otherwise empty scene.

Hilda Carline *Hill Farm, Wangford*, 1925, oil on canvas, 34 × 87cm (below).

At the start of the 1880s, two ancient foes – the elegant town of Southwold and the still ramshackle fishing village of Walberswick – seemed in danger of losing a shared and new-found reputation. The seaside settlements, which had long glared at each other across the slowly closing mouth of the River Blyth, had lately merged in spirit as a haven for painters. Now, however, foul development was afoot.

The *Punch* illustrator Charles Keene had grown up largely in Ipswich, and he retained a life-long affection for the distinctive scenery of Suffolk. In particular, from the 1860s, he sketched as he wandered the shifting coastline between Southwold and the crumbling cliffs above the drowned medieval port of Dunwich. Much of what he depicted has itself proved transient. Word spread. The English marine painter Henry Moore also came to work in the then-remote area, trailing lesser talents in his wake. But the 1881 issue of *The Etcher* offered an obituarist's tribute to such scenic taste: two views of Southwold harbour – one by Keene, the other by T. I. Dalgleish – were accompanied by a mournful commentary. It was suggested that, in addition to the silt that had almost sealed the harbour, the arrival of the railway from Halesworth, via Wenhaston, Blythburgh and Walberswick, surely signalled the doom of Southwold as a fertile sketching ground. The epitaph ended by noting a lack of colour at Walberswick, owing to

Philip Wilson Steer *Self Portrait*, **1920, oil on canvas, 74 × 59cm.**

the black tarred roofs of the fishermen's shacks. However, in the ensuing decade the village came to support a thriving colony of artists, the greatest among them being a sparkling colourist named **Philip Wilson Steer** (1860-1942).

Since his father was a painter of landscapes and portraits in a mediocre eighteenth-century manner, the young Steer gained an early artistic education to match his conventional upbringing. He trained in Paris after being rejected by the Royal Academy Schools; but, apart from a revelatory introduction to the work of Manet, it may have been on tours of London galleries that the introverted student became infused with the daring ideas of Impressionism. Wherever Steer had found his guiding light, when he returned from France in 1884, he seems to have headed straight for Walberswick. And there, making lengthy and almost annual visits until 1891, he translated the language of the revolutionary French artists, and reworked references to Whistler, to create a painterly vocabulary of his own.

At first he probably stayed at an inn on the green which has since been converted into a private house; later he lodged at Valley Farm, on the north-eastern edge of the village. On several occasions he was accompanied by Fred Brown, the painter and teacher who became director of the Slade in 1892. Painting trips were also taken to Southwold, which was soon within easy reach of Walberswick thanks to the new River Blyth Ferry Company. From the evidence of surviving sketchbooks, Steer liked to walk around the area, taking down lightning notes in pencil and black crayon to build up a picture of atmosphere and place. Quick oil sketches on panels gave further detail. This catalogue of colour and composition would then be called upon for the final oil painting, produced perhaps months or possibly years afterwards in the artist's London studio.

By the early 1890s, a parade of glittering seaside pictures had earned Steer a reputation as the most 'ultra' painter of his day. His work incited hostility – being branded both 'crudely horrid' and an 'aggressive affectation'; but this courteous artist was free of all dogma and any desire to shock. Radically changing technique at several points in his career, he employed stylistic devices that seemed most suited for the subject and the mood he wished to convey. Thus the dazzling, dancing interplay of sun, sea and shore at Walberswick was best captured by the broken brushstrokes and the vivid, unmixed colours of Impressionism – as was the image of fleeting youth. Many of Steer's Suffolk studies featured young girls in bright clothes, bathing, playing or gazing enigmatically out to sea. One model has been identified as a local fisherman's daughter, Dolly Brown (later to marry the portrait painter Frank Morley Fletcher), who tripped across several pictures in a pink or white dress, black stockings and a scarlet sash.

The painting *Knucklebones* was first exhibited in 1889, three years after Steer had helped to found the Francophile New English Art Club as a rival to the conservative Royal Academy. Superficially it seemed to be a clever copy of Gallic 'dot and dab' innovation:

the composition of the children echoes Degas, the curling brushstrokes at the water's edge Monet and the somewhat unscientific 'pointillist' colouring of the shingle Seurat. Amid such probable influences, however, Steer emerges as his own man. Everything is orchestrated to create the 'unity of vision' the artist sought. The overall effect is of carefree days in the endless summers of memory. He strove to go beyond the immediacy of the moment to create a poetic

Philip Wilson Steer *Bathing Tents, Walberswick*, c. 1888, oil on board, 20 × 25cm.

Philip Wilson Steer *Two Girls on a Beach*, c. 1884, oil on canvas, 25 × 54cm.

Philip Wilson Steer
Girls Running, **oil on canvas,**
63 × 93cm.

image tinged with nostalgia. It is tempting to speculate that such a quality arose from the artist's recollection of high summer in Suffolk while working in wintry Chelsea.

This proposition seems at its most convincing when applied to *Girls Running, Walberswick.* Here the strong colour of the group at the end of the pier helps to make the delicate figures in the foreground still less substantial and more eerily dream-like. The heavily reworked picture also hints at the agonies the artist suffered to secure his calm images. Indeed, so pitted and pummelled is the paint surface that it resembles the sand at Walberswick after pelting rain. And *pentimenti* – where later layers of paint have become transparent with age – show that the two girls were originally holding hands. Their shadows on the pier are still true to this position.

Perhaps the finest evocation of a sun-drenched beach scene is *Children Paddling, Walberswick,* which takes themes and motifs from earlier pictures to new heights of harmony. In a triumph of colour, the

brilliant blue of the sea is complemented by a splash of warm red dress, lilac sails and the creamy-white uniting sand and sunlight on the water. But again, cracks betray the complex evolution of this enchanting study. The key central figure was certainly a late addition to the party: fissures in the red paint of her skirt reveal beach colours underneath.

But if this painting was a peak it was also a point of departure; for, by the mid-1890s, Steer's artistic direction was to alter dramatically. He began to re-assess the classic British landscape tradition – notably the style of Constable and the subjects of Turner. Such a move may have been impelled by commercial motives. William Rothenstein, visiting the artist at this time, saw a studio filled with unsold pictures of 'yachts and the sea, and of girls with long legs like Sheraton tables'.

The sylph-like girls lingered on, but Steer sought different ways of painting as he set about exploring the diversity of the English landscape. He made brief return trips to East Anglia, staying at

Harwich in 1914 and 1929, and Framlingham in 1928. Reinterpreting Whistler in late watercolours, as his eyesight began to fade, he stripped nature back to its most elemental expanses of sky, sea and land, using a minimum of washed-out, closely linked tones. The reserved artist had retreated from the bold beauty of his Walberswick images, to a masterly under-statement that seemed most in tune with his temperament.

Moving forward to the late summer of 1914, over two decades after Philip Wilson Steer's final departure, two more fascinating figures could be observed at Walberswick. A man and woman of middle years and faded fortune, they worked each day in a cramped studio by the river, emerging in the evening to take long walks across the dunes, heath and marshes. They claimed to be searching for flowers, but the locals were suspicious. Other artists were packing up for the season: an annual migration had been accelerated by the outbreak of war. But these two strangers showed no sign of leaving. Worse still, they were known to exchange letters with a revolutionary group in Austria. Amid a threat of invasion, and stringent security regulations all along the coast, the good folk of Walberswick were fired by fear and patriotic duty to suspect the presence of spies.

Charles Rennie Mackintosh (1868-1928) and his wife Margaret were, in fact, fleeing from a rejection of their creative ideas in Glasgow. From the 1890s, together with Margaret's sister and brother-in-law, they had made the city one of Europe's key

Philip Wilson Steer *Children Paddling*, 1894, oil on canvas, 64 × 92cm.

Philip Wilson Steer
***Knucklebones, Walberswick*, 1888-9, oil on canvas.**

centres of artistic innovation, embracing the Arts and Crafts Movement and the incoming influence of Art Nouveau. But Mackintosh, a superlative architect, designer and painter, had outshone all others, before fashions changed and the jealousy of inferior talents bit. As commissions dried up, a whispering campaign gathered force, alleging that the demon drink had left the great man unable to complete a simple drawing. In a crisis of confidence, he ran away – to Walberswick. Far from the solace he had hoped for, however, he found himself beset by further vicious rumour; but revenge, both sad and sweet, was due.

In his Suffolk hideaway Mackintosh soon proved his detractors wrong, producing several elegant and assured watercolours of the harbour area. And, with the promise of a book to be published in Germany, he began work on a remarkable series of flower studies. Architectural training had developed the artist's facility as a draughtsman. Moreover, nature – and especially wildflowers – had inspired much of his furniture and decoration. In early notebooks he had drawn both plants and details of vernacular buildings, to construct a design vocabulary. But by the time of a 1905 visit to Blakeney, the flowers had become coloured, stylised and outstanding in their own right: at Walberswick they would reach their fullest bloom.

Rapidly sketching fine specimens as he found them, Mackintosh captured with a firm and flowing line the life of the growing plant: until leaving Suffolk he abhorred cut flowers. Then, indoors,

FRANCIS NEWBERY (1853-1946) used his influence when director of the Glasgow School of Art to promote Mackintosh and his circle. And it was he who encouraged the idea of a bolt-hole on the Suffolk coast. Newbery and his wife Jessie – a gifted embroidery designer – rented a house in Walberswick each summer as a base for sketching and painting. After their flight from Scotland, Margaret and Charles Rennie Mackintosh took rooms next door.

Francis Newbery *A View from a Window, Walberswick*, 1912, oil on canvas, 60 × 44cm (right).

Other Scottish artists attracted to the Walberswick area at this time included one of the 'Glasgow Boys', Edward Arthur Walton, and the draughtsman and etcher David Muirhead Bone.

Charles Rennie Mackintosh, photographed in 1893.

transparent washes were applied to the drawing, and specific sections might be picked out in solid colour. Each design, almost Japanese in its formal elegance, would then be completed by the careful positioning of a cartouche containing Mackintosh's initials, the subject, date and place name. An added 'MMM' indicated that Margaret had helped with the invariably exquisite colouring.

But local hatreds were hardening. It could not have been an unfamiliar accent that aroused such mistrust for, since the founding of the Southwold Harbour Company in 1906, the briefly flourishing herring industry had brought an influx of fish-gutting girls from Scotland who were ferried daily between work and lodgings at Walberswick. But war was no climate for watercolourists, particularly those prone to nocturnal wanderings and to corres-pondence with radical artists of the Viennese Secession. Returning one evening, the couple found a soldier guarding their rented rooms. Mackintosh was accused of being an enemy agent and summoned to appear before a tribunal. Only after a lengthy delay, while influential friends appealed to the War Office, was the charge lifted. The artists then flew once more, first to London and finally to France.

Charles Rennie Mackintosh did not live to see his work return to fashion. The hoped-for botanical book was ruled out by the war, and when peace came the cost of publication in Britain was judged prohibitive. The 30 or so unbound leaves, executed at Walberswick in barely a year, were scattered. In exile, Mackintosh continued to develop unique but unnoticed watercolours of landscape, still lifes and flowers. He died in London, having undergone

Charles Rennie Mackintosh
Walberswick, 1915, watercolour,
28 × 38cm.

treatment for cancer of the tongue, in December 1928. Margaret died four years later.

Ten years after Mackintosh's death, as another war loomed, the writer and painter **Adrian Stokes** (1902-72) and the artist **Margaret Mellis** (b. 1914) were house-hunting further along the Suffolk coast. Having several times visited Walberswick, Stokes had asked a friend to let him know if a particular property became vacant: but he was out of luck. Instead, the couple inspected a martello tower near Aldeburgh, on a narrowing peninsula between the river and the sea (a surrounding village, Slaughden, was by this time washed away). Margaret thought it dungeon-like and Adrian worried that the track from Aldeburgh was threatened by shingle drifts. And anyway, Margaret preferred the rugged coastline of Cornwall, where the perfect house was finally located, overlooking the beach at Carbis Bay. That find may have changed the course of English art.

After Munich, Adrian Stokes was convinced that London would be destroyed by bombs in an imminent war. He and Margaret chose their evacuees in advance; and in the dying days of 1939, Ben Nicholson, his wife Barbara Hepworth, their triplets, a nursemaid and a cook, duly arrived. Other visitors included Victor Pasmore and William Coldstream, while the constructivist Naum Gabo and his wife went to live nearby. Nicholson went on to incorporate aspects of local landscapes into his seemingly abstract paintings, to teach Peter Lanyon and to influence the next wave of artists drawn to the St Ives area including Hilton, Heron, Frost and Wynter. Hepworth remained based in Cornwall for the rest of her life.

How much East Anglia might have gained if only that house at Walberswick had been available!

Charles Rennie Mackintosh *Fritillaria*, **1915, pencil and watercolour, 25 × 20cm (opposite).**

Francis Davison *Green Star*, **collage, 124 × 131cm.**

Margaret Mellis *Resurrection*,
1985, construction in wood,
46 × 23 × 22cm.

Margaret Mellis *Four Angels*,
1986, construction in wood,
32 × 65 × 5cm.

The clarity of the coastal light in Suffolk rivals that of Cornwall; the horizons are wider. But perhaps the flat, wide-open eastern landscape is less conducive to a clustering of creative talent. And, in truth, the West Country had long lured: Whistler and Sickert had raised the reputation of St Ives in the 1880s, and Alfred Munnings was among the artists who visited Newlyn early this century. Moreover, Ben Nicholson and Christopher Wood had delighted in a 1928 stay in St Ives.

In 1946, the Stokes' marriage came to grief. After Adrian left, Patrick and Delia Heron went to stay with Margaret at Carbis Bay; and they, in turn, invited a recently divorced friend named **Francis Davison** (1919-84). Margaret and Francis struck up an immediate friendship, married in 1948 and were rarely parted thereafter. The couple spent three years living in the Davison chateau on the Cap d'Antibes, before returning to England – to Walberswick, where a friend had offered to rent them a fisherman's shed. This time the countryside found favour, though the hut did not: a small inheritance allowed the purchase of a cottage and four-acre smallholding at Syleham, near Diss. For the next 25 years they lived frugally by keeping fowls (first in a box under the kitchen table), selling eggs and growing barley and vegetables. Margaret, resolutely creative, developed the paintings and constructions so admired by Nicholson and Gabo; Francis proceeded to simplify his semi-representational pictures into landscapes of fewer and flatter shapes until arriving at abstract collage.

At first, since brightly coloured papers were not yet available, hues appeared muted, and restrained themes and rhythms were worked out between relatively simple marshallings of forms. But Davison was slowly building a brilliant feel for the torn edge and for tone. The strictest limits of the medium suited the artist's astringency: he used scissors less and less and never applied paint. But here were also strong references to the austerity of the East Anglian landscape. The hue and patterning of farm buildings, and of fields dissected by paths and hedges, resonate through this work. The critic Julian Spalding, who was first alerted to the power of the collages by Mary Potter, says: 'The sensation one has is of walking through a landscape, with everything in flux, changing about you.' His work might also be said to evoke the countryside as perceived by a bird in flight.

By the mid-1970s, the ravages of inflation and fowlpest had made life at Syleham untenable. Helped by Margaret's sister, the couple moved to an almost gardenless house on a green at Southwold. Although the underlying structure and design always held firm, Davison's subsequent collages saw a burst of glowing colours and ever larger, more complex and more agitated arrangements of shapes: thus the move from an isolated smallholding to a lively seaside resort was felt in the work. By the time he died, of a brain tumour, he had enjoyed a retrospective exhibition at London's Hayward Gallery, but otherwise his art remained undiscovered. Francis Davison now lies buried at Walberswick.

Margaret Mellis continues as a prolific and substantial artist, now embracing many changes of media: in dead flower studies of the 1950s she expressed a sense of loss; and most recently an un-conscious theme of resurrection has been played out through semi-figurative constructions and reliefs. But as the painter Patrick Heron comments: 'The great optimism which dedication to sheer colour and form always generates in painting is a permanent charac-teristic of all Margaret's work, of whatever period. Qualities of robust strength, both of colour and execution, together with an apparent simplicity of construction – these also are permanent features.'

She collects driftwood, discarded boards once used to flatten herring for kippering and even eroded timbers from nearby Blythburgh Church. Into her constructed landscapes she cuts the suggested shape of a man, often set against his hollow absence. And in such celebratory marriages of form and colour her optimism survives.

Francis Davison *Black landscape,* **collage on board, 63 × 76cm.**

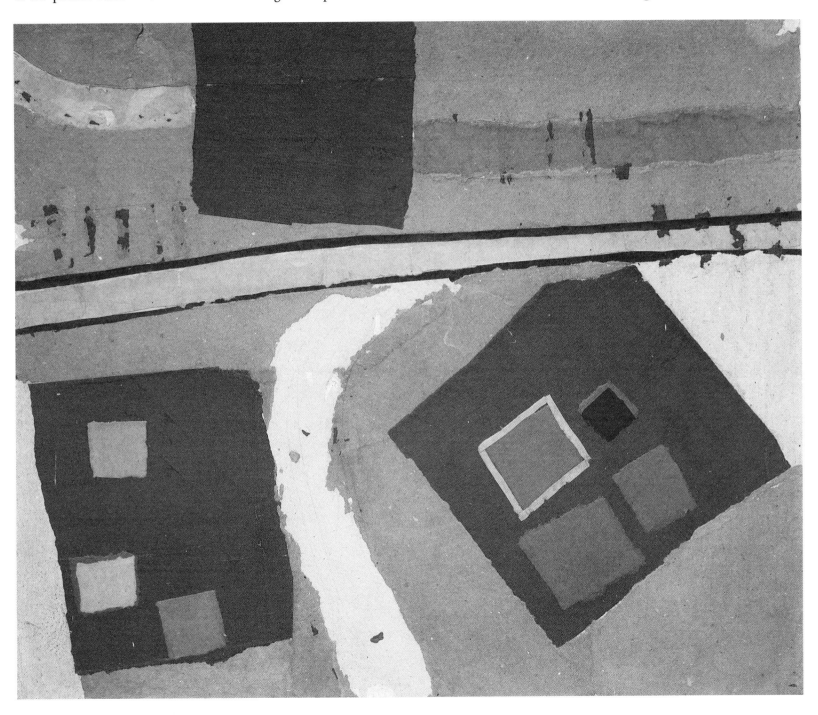

O happy the farmer and free from all care
Who rises each morning to breathe fresh air
And hears the birds singing from every
green bough.
No life like the farmer who follows the plough.

(Traditional)

Harry Becker *Man Hedging,* **oil on board, 38 × 46cm.**

To anyone arriving in north-east Suffolk just before the First World War, the popular rhymers' image of bucolic bliss would have seemed at odds with the evidence of the unkempt cottages before him; still more so with the overgrown fields beyond. Save for a brief respite during the Boer War, agriculture had been in decline for more than three decades. Borne down by cheap imports from the New World, English farm incomes had plummeted – with the price of wheat alone cut by half – and millions of acres had been taken out of production. Arable East Anglia had been worst affected. **Harry Becker** (1865-1928), who arrived with his wife and daughter in Wenhaston in 1913, noted more hardship than

happiness in faithful records of rural life in this corner of Suffolk.

Becker was born in Colchester, one of four sons of a German immigrant doctor. His artistic talent was recognised early: at 14 he went to the Royal Academy Schools at Antwerp, and then, from 1884, to the Paris studio of the popular portrait painter Carolus Duran (who also taught John Singer Sargent). Although copying Duran's theories of tonality, he also admired the techniques of the Impressionists which his tutor scorned – Degas, in particular, would prove a lasting influence. On returning to Colchester, the emergent artist lived at The Minories, painting tentative oil studies and watercolour portraits and landscapes in a style derived from Duran. Then, in 1894, he left for London.

In the capital, Becker slowly established a reputation as a lithographer, while potboiler portraits, historical works and posters paid the bills. The key personal event of this period was his marriage to the

Harry Becker *The Scyther*, 1913, lithograph, 96 × 56cm.

FOR **CHARLES KEENE** (1823-91), the Victorian illustrator, Dunwich was the finest spot in his favourite county of Suffolk. He returned there again and again to draw and to play the bagpipes to the sea that had swallowed up a bustling port, complete with almost 20 churches, chapels and monasteries. His skill and honesty as a draughtsman were hailed by the Impressionists yet scarcely recognised in England. In 1883 Pissarro wrote to his son Lucien: 'England has Keene, he does not exhibit, he is not fashionable, and that is everything. England, like France, is rotten to the core, she knows only one art, the art of throwing sand in your eyes.' But Keene's lack of acclaim was in part self-imposed: contented, unambitious and more than a little eccentric, he was indifferent to wordly success. Away from London, he rejoiced in solitude, as he made plain in a letter to the artist Joseph Crawhall:

'This Dunwich is a curious little place, but interesting. All along at the base of the sandy cliff (striped with layers of rolled pebbles) you come upon human bones that have dropped from the shallow alluvial soil at the top. The land is sinking all along the coast, and a great city that flourished in Saxon times and was decaying at the Norman Conquest [*sic*] lies miles under the sea. There is one ruined church left just at the edge of the cliff. I believe the "oldest inhabitant" can just remember when it was used for a service, but its only congregation now is the owls and bats! . . . My bag pipes are "going" well just now from the practice I've had in my holiday, and so secluded is this place that at any time two or three hundred yards down the beach I can strut on the hard sand and skirl away at "Fingal's Lament" or "The Massacre of Glencoe" (my favourite pibroch) out of earshot of a soul.'

The church that Charles Keene depicted, All Saints, was lost in the present century: in 1904 the east end tumbled down the cliffs and what remained of the tower followed in 1919.

Charles Keene *Coast View with Ruins of Old Church, Dunwich*, etching, 14 × 18cm.

painter Georgina Waddington in 1902. Several trips were paid to the flatlands of East Anglia, Kent and Holland, during which compositions of rural workers were evoked with a growing lightness of touch and an immediacy of expression. The artist had at last found his subject.

But he pressed on with conflicting commissions in London, notably an order, accepted in 1908, to execute giant murals of farm labourers for the new Selfridges store. Full-sized cartoons for the project had already been completed when a dispute with Gordon Selfridge brought work to an abrupt halt. The surviving studies, with figures verging on the heroic, contrast sharply with the rest of Becker's drawn-from-life peasant portraits. This episode also confirmed the artist's contempt for patronage, recognition and the commercial art world. During his London years he showed at leading galleries, especially the Royal Academy, as well as in Venice and Milan; but he was involved in no artists' groups and

Harry Becker *Cutting Chaff in the Open*, **oil on board, 46 × 38cm.**

spurned any idea of self-promotion. Although painters such as Sargent and Frank Brangwyn bought his work, he was never part of their world. And, in 1913, at the age of 48, he withdrew into rural isolation.

First at Wenhaston, and later at Hinton, near Darsham, Harry Becker would follow his farm-worker neighbours into the fields in the early morning, and with speed and fluency set down the patterns of their labour in notes, sketches and large-scale paintings. For lithographs, he had huge blocks of stone hauled after him, to be drawn on out of doors. His most ambitious effort – a 1915 London Underground poster designed to attract city girls to war-time land work (perhaps noticed by Hilda Carline) – had entailed the carting of a block said to weigh half a ton. By such exhausting means he nevertheless managed to echo the Impressionist aim of capturing the moment. His remarkable range of media embraced etching, pencil, charcoal, pen-and-ink, chalk, pastels, watercolour and oils.

Sharing the hours, food and gossip of the labourers, Becker also experienced their poverty. A meagre income was provided by Georgina, who, having selflessly abandoned her own ambition to paint, taught art at St Felix School, Southwold. With little money for materials, Harry worked on the backs of sketches by his wife's pupils, greaseproof paper, sacking; luminous oils were produced on paper sprayed with paraffin. But commissions or chance sales remained unwelcome. 'I think it's so disheartening to give away your pictures', he said, 'because then they're hung on the walls and nobody ever looks at them again.' When funds allowed he even bought works back.

The artist's achievement was to record without sentimentality, and with a rare economy of means, a vanishing way of life. His lean figures may exude an almost classical grace, but they are clearly engaged in back-breaking toil; in contrast to the sleek creatures depicted by Munnings, his horses are scrawny and stiff-legged. The onlooker is always aware of the weather, which blows and drenches but still allows the glorious spectacle of a sun setting into a vast pink East Anglian sky.

Soon after Becker moved to Suffolk, war revived farm fortunes (while inciting petty prejudice against an artist of German ancestry). Peace, which saw memorials replacing maypoles on countless village greens, brought a fresh slump. When Becker's

Harry Becker *Harvest*, 1922, **lithograph, 104 × 127cm.**

subjects were not being drafted into the trenches, low wages forced them to seek work in the cities. And the march of mechanisation was gaining in step. Although English farms retained a million horses early in the century, steam advanced rapidly: corn could now be cut and bound into sheaves by a single machine. Railways opened even the remotest East Anglian farming communities to the outside world. Becker's studies were completed in the nick of time.

For an artist who never sought it, due tribute came posthumously, when the Suffolk writer Adrian Bell chose works by Becker to illustrate 1940s editions of his rural trilogy – *The Cherry Tree, Silver Ley* and *Corduroy*. These, too, were reminders of something that had all but gone.

As the wound of the First World War deepened, others sought to get away from it all in East Anglia. Early in 1916, the conscription of men without dependants, and aged between 18 and 41, sent conscientious objectors searching for work of 'national importance' on the land. Pacifists among the Bloomsbury Group artists joined the quest.

The painter **Duncan Grant** (1885-1978) moved to Wissett Lodge near Halesworth, which had been owned by a recently deceased aunt. He and the writer David Garnett attempted to cultivate six acres of overgrown land, including unkempt orchards and sickly blackcurrant bushes. Their amateur efforts met with local disdain, and neighbours were outraged when, as a defence against theft, the pair painted the tails of their white leghorn chickens blue. Soon **Vanessa Bell** (1879-1961) arrived, along with her two sons, a nursemaid and cook. An artistic colony had taken root.

At this time, Grant and Bell were at the height of their painterly powers. Looking to Paris, and revering Cézanne, they had become leading English proponents of 'modernism'. Their palettes were never richer, nor their brush strokes more lively, as they set about creating form from pure colour. Key members of Roger Fry's Omega Workshops, both had become adept at vivacious decoration – covering walls,

Ivon Hitchens *Suffolk Marshes*,
1933, oil on canvas, 54 × 60cm.

IVON HITCHENS (1893-1979) is best known for his meditations on the ponds, birch groves and bracken of a tranquil corner of Sussex where he lived from 1940. But during the 1930s he had a retreat on the north Suffolk coast, at Sizewell, and painted rural scenes across the county.

It was at Sizewell that John Piper met his second wife, Myfanwy Evans, in the summer of 1934. Their host was the only painter to remain a member of the Seven and Five Society from start to finish (1919-35) – during which time he produced the lyrical, semi-naive landscapes often associated with that fast-changing group. He painted at Higham in the Stour Valley, while staying with the artists Ida and Blair Hughes-Stanton; and honeymooned at Sizewell, in 1935, after marrying Mary Cranford Coates. But only towards the close of the 1930s, when Hitchens had ended a brief flirtation with abstraction – and was painting Holbrook pools to the south of Ipswich and a path through a Suffolk wood during stays on the Shotley Peninsula – were the main motifs of his career beginning to emerge.

With great sweeps of housepainters' brushes, Ivon Hitchens would evoke the sensation of the landscape before him – the feel, colour and pattern of an environment, filtered through his own personality and the process of constructing a study on canvas. He said: 'A picture is compounded of three parts – one part artist, one part nature, one part the work itself. All three should sing together.'

artefacts and furniture with vivid hues. During a 1913 camping holiday at Brandon, for instance, Vanessa executed a sketch of figures and tents in a wooded landscape, which prompted the design of a striking fire screen. Wissett Lodge was itself turned into a work of art. The walls of the house were drenched in blue distemper, and then adorned with a riot of figures and forms (murals echoing Fra Angelico

graced one bedroom); when they came to leave, however, the painters had to remove all trace of their 'shocking' taste.

Only on Sundays was Grant free to consider canvases inspired by local subjects, whereas Bell spent several hours each day in her studio. She painted a view from her window of a farm pond, with a distinctive Omega jug placed on the foreground sill.

Vanessa Bell *The Pond*, c.1916, oil on canvas, 63 × 67cm.

A window-framed glimpse of garden or landscape became a recurring motif in her work, satisfying, as it did, a modernist desire for a flattened picture plane and private, domestic concerns. From spartan surroundings, Vanessa created an atmosphere of warmth and well-being which lulled the restless talents that converged around her. Her sister, Virginia Woolf, wrote after visiting Wissett: 'I've seldom enjoyed myself more than I did with you, and I can't make out exactly how you manage. One seems to get into such a contented state of mind. I heard from Lytton [Strachey] who feels the same, and says he would like to live with you forever.' Following her trip to Suffolk, she conceived the first ideas for her novel *Night and Day*, with a central character based on Vanessa.

Yet the prospect of prison threatened this oasis of calm. Grant and Garnett were called before Blything Tribunal and, even though their advocates included the economist Maynard Keynes, the panel of farmers was unmoved. An Appeal Tribunal in Ipswich proved more sympathetic, and exemption from military service was granted; but the Central Tribunal later ruled that although the two men could engage in farm work, they could not be self-employed. Thus, the Bloomsbury household shifted from Suffolk to Sussex – to Charleston, where Bell and Grant were to be based for the rest of their lives.

Another Bloomsbury visitor was **Roger Fry** (1866-1934), who gained a first class honours degree in natural sciences at King's College, Cambridge, before taking up the study and practice of art. Painting at Blythburgh during the summers of 1892 and 1893, he produced one particularly impressive oil, in which the estuary unwinds behind bold silhouettes of foreground trees. Frances Spalding, Fry's biographer, suspects it was to this picture the artist referred when in 1912 he informed the critic D. S. MacColl: 'One of my earliest oil-paintings was essentially Post-Impressionist, but was so derided at the time – I never showed it publicly – that I gave in to what I thought were wiser counsels and my next rebellion against the dreary naturalism of my youth lay in the direction of archaism.' Late in 1893, Fry had underlined his feelings in a letter to his father. 'I am repainting most of my Suffolk pictures', he wrote, 'as I found they were too detailed and literal and that for the final effect I must get away from nature.' Eclectic in the extreme, his art was never as daring as the Post-Impressionists he was to champion in the criticism that made his name.

Towards the end of his life, he persuaded his lover, Helen Anrep, to purchase a house in Suffolk, where the light and lie of the land reminded him of Holland. Rodwell House, at Claydon, near Ipswich, was later to welcome the founders of the Euston Road School of Art, William Coldstream, Victor Pasmore and Claude Rogers. Fry adored it. He bought a battered Citroën and, armed with unbridled optimism and a map, would trek cross country to take in the local sights (once informing Vanessa Bell of a journey through a field of mustard, 'I find that a motor will go on No 1 gear almost anywhere').

In 1930 Roger Fry finally secured the Slade professorship at Cambridge. His portrait by Vanessa Bell, first shown at London's Lefevre Gallery as a memorial tribute, now hangs in his old college.

Vanessa Bell *Portrait of Roger Fry*, 1933, oil on canvas, 70 × 54cm.

Aldeburgh holds on to a strip of marsh, extending inland to Snape, like a life-line. Without it, the home town of the poet George Crabbe, generations of fishermen and a celebrated arts festival would be an island. Small wonder that water has pervaded the work of many painters, both residents and visitors here.

Meres, marshy streams and woodland pools – and a silver-grey sea merging sky and shingle – washed over the pictures of **Mary Potter** (1900-81). Her increasingly abstract and allusive work, with its muted tones and diluted forms, seems to suggest survivals from a drowned world. It is no coincidence that wave-lapped Aldeburgh was the artist's adopted town for the last 30 years of her life.

Born Mary Attenborough, in Beckenham, she upset her middle-class parents by single-mindedly selecting painting from many talents. Again and again she showed courage and confidence. At the Slade her determination to work in pale tones was rewarded with a first prize for portrait painting and a place in a New English Art Club exhibition. But just when skill and a gregarious nature had secured success as a portraitist, she felt she was working to a formula: the thickly-painted faces in her studio were ceremonially burned. Later, when married to the writer Stephen Potter, mother of two children and organiser of a series of war-time homes all over the country, the artist displayed similar resolve to pursue her work as she wished.

While living by the Thames, at Chiswick, from 1927, Mary Potter had begun to dabble with the watery vision she would explore for the rest of her life. She was an early member of the London Group, and showed brief allegiance to the Seven and Five Society, but always charted an individual course. And though some saw a passion for Pierro della Francesca, Gwen John and Chinese art – and later for Braque, Klee and Matisse – reflected in her pictures, the spare lyricism of her paint was entirely new. Frequent visits

Mary Potter *The Mere*, **1958, oil on canvas, 50 × 76cm.**

Mary Potter *Sun in Water,* 1979,
oil on canvas, 127 × 152cm.

to the sea culminated in 1951, when the Potter family moved to The Red House, on the edge of Aldeburgh. The Suffolk fishing port was to supply the inspiration for Mary's finest art and, especially after her divorce in 1955, a great friendship with the founders of the Aldeburgh Festival, Benjamin Britten and Peter Pears. Indeed, they swapped homes in 1955 and, for six years, the painter worked from Crag House on the seafront, before a live-in studio took shape in The Red House gardens. Here, apart from holidays and occasional visits from painter friends such as Prunella Clough, John Piper and Sidney Nolan, Mary Potter used her isolation to continue thinning her paint and paring down her vision – blurring outlines and details, even abolishing the horizon line altogether. Paradoxically, she worked on ever larger canvases, which seemed to mirror her growing acclaim.

Many pictures are underlain by a rectilinear structure, suggesting the window through which a solitary artist viewed the world. Sometimes there are framed patches of landscape, or a square of North Sea; and perhaps flowers, a jug or paint brushes in a jar have been placed on a sill. Other works comprise compositions from studio objects: lamps, furniture, crockery, shells. It is an intensely personal world, made more poignant by that masterly understatement. 'What isn't there', the artist once said, 'matters most.'

CLAUDE ROGERS (1907-79) trained at the Slade in the 1920s, as well as working in Paris. He was one of the quartet of artists who founded and ran London's Euston Road School, between 1937 and the outbreak of World War Two, which was close to Sickert's earlier Camden Town Group in every sense. With Victor Pasmore, William Coldstream and Graham Bell, he rejected the 'vociferation and pretentious flourish' of the Surrealists, advocating instead the 'humility and honesty' that came from objective appraisal of the real world. Opposing extreme modernism, he sought a return to the art of observation. 'The result', Frances Spalding has written, 'was a lyrical realism, socially inspired but aesthetically conceived, and which, in its economy and restraint, is peculiarly English, reticent yet poetic.'

Claude Rogers *Aldeburgh Beach,*
oil on canvas, 51 × 61cm.

The 1930s also saw Rogers visiting Suffolk, staying at Claydon, near Ipswich, and working on the coast. This painter in oils in traditional fields – landscapes, portraits and still lifes – developed a gentle passion for the atmosphere of East Anglia. Faithful to his own teaching, he portrayed true-to-life subjects: a Suffolk bus stop, burning stubble, a quarry, fishing boats and day trippers on Aldeburgh beach. In later years he had a house at Somerton, mid-way between Sudbury and Bury St Edmunds. Between teaching terms, he found inspiration in such sights as the view towards the village of Hartest, a pond or a combine harvester. And, having started with a subdued palette, he developed an increasing interest in colour.

The critic who praised Mary Potter's 'no-man's-land' palette was right in several senses. An astonishing range of pale-toned and opalescent colours – lilac, pinks, yellows, blues, faint olive-green, browns – was uniquely hers, while a predominance of greys hinted at a gentle melancholy. And, whether flooded with light or pervaded by a luminous mist like a gauzy material, the prevailing atmosphere is utterly feminine.

When working out a painting, the artist would often use as a starting point one or two watercolours, perhaps of landscapes completed while sitting in her car. Or else she relied on memory, which may have enhanced a hazy, dream-like quality in the finished work. And throughout, the essences of past and private experience were transformed into universal meaning, rather in the way that a leaf frozen in amber tells of a primeval forest about which there is no other sign.

Kenneth Clark said that Mary Potter's delicate pictures 'exist in the domain of seeing and feeling; we

Mary Potter *Sun on the Beach*, **1961, oil on canvas, 82 × 93cm.**

IN THE 1950s, when playwrights like John Osborne were looking back in anger, their painter contemporaries were portraying the grim social reality of the kitchen sink. **Peter Coker** (b. London, 1926) extended the idea in a series of paintings, using thick pigment to depict slabs, hooks and carcasses of the butcher's shop. With such unsqueamish works, the former St Martin's School of Art and Royal College student made his name. But he has proved his depth and virtuosity in later landscapes, particularly after a move to East Anglia in 1962.

Installed at The Red House, Mistley, above the Stour estuary, he analysed in several series of drawings and paintings the English wooded landscape, inspired by trips to the Tunstall and Rendlesham forests. His colours were subdued or sombre; through bare trunks and branches he struck a dramatic, even elegiac note. As Frederick Gore remarks: 'He instinctively seeks subjects which reveal powerful forces at work – physical situations of an elemental kind which have strong psychic correspondences.' It seems only natural, therefore, that Coker was to be moved by the power of the North Sea pounding the shingle at Aldeburgh. His fundamental pictures – some from a viewpoint behind a balcony, catching the varying light in a room, on the beach and playing on the open sea – have been expressed through an increasing economy of design. 'Through the study of water,' Gore adds, 'Coker has been led not only to investigate the forces recorded in the solid substances of our environment but also the forces we see at work – from the movement of water to the movement of the weather and so to atmosphere and light.'

Over time, the palette of this Royal Academician (elected 1972) has lightened and brightened markedly. His paint has thinned, his brushwork has become freer. He has ranged ever further afield, painting the immensity of northern skies and the intensity of summer in the Mediterranean. But East Anglia remains his greatest love. 'The landscape is just as good [as France]', he says, 'and the light is quite extraordinary.'

Peter Coker *Aldeburgh*, 1964, oil on board, 122 × 122cm.

know that they are exactly right in the same way that we know a singer to be perfectly in tune. Yet just as the purest voice still has a human inflection, so these pure visual responses would move us less were they not also a revelation of character.' His conclusion that the paintings are 'enchanting moments of heightened perception' should stand as the artist's epitaph.

Living close to Mary Potter in later life was a lyrical painter 18 years her junior, whose star had shone briefly very early on. The *Birmingham Post* of 8th June 1928 had been moved to comment: 'Sir John

Lavery opened Miss Peggy Somerville's exhibition of drawings, watercolours and oils today at the Claridge Galleries, when the artist wore a tiny muslin frock, white socks and sandals, and hair à la Goldilocks.'

At the tender age of ten **Peggy Somerville** (1918-75) had caused a sensation. Her first solo show saw a chic London gallery all but besieged. A display of more than 100 pictures was soon sold out and replacements were hurriedly ordered. Rave reviews reverberated around the world. The society portraitist Lavery, also listed among the buyers, was much echoed when declaring himself 'completely mystified by the little girl's genius'. But there had been fair warning: the artist exhibited her first works at the Royal Drawing Society – minute landscapes shimmering with yellow, pink and grey washes – when three years old. And in 1927, New Irish Salon judges applauded a bold and breezy oil entitled *Happy Days by the Sea*, unaware that its creator was not yet nine.

Born Margaret Scott Somerville, Peggy began to draw as soon as she was able to hold a pencil. A posthumous exhibition at the Norwich Castle Museum – which has a major collection of the artist's work – displayed a sheet of the three-year-old child's miniature scenes and tiny watercolour tin, with its squares of pigment almost worn away. She was an infant prodigy but never a precocious child; instead,

Peggy Somerville at work, aged three, and *Sunset*, a mature work completed when she was seven, oil on canvas, 10 × 13cm.

she was shy and diffident, and painted with complete unselfconsciousness. Her training came from watching her father and her elder brother Stuart – both were accomplished artists – and from working by instinct alone in the garden or among gypsy caravans by the river. Not that she cared for direct copies of nature, saying of her swiftly-sketched work: 'I see the picture in my mind and then just paint it.' These distillations of memory and imagination were to last all her life.

A sureness of technique, composition and vision – coupled with a childish freshness and spontaneity of painting – gave Peggy three solo exhibitions in London by the time she had turned 14, and had moved with her family from Middlesex to south-west Suffolk. Each was a triumph. Critics and fellow painters saved special praise for her mastery of colour. At the third show, Sickert did more than recognise a kindred spirit: he purchased *The White Horse* and pronounced it 'one of the finest landscapes yet painted by a [living] English artist'. But public acclaim and unwelcome celebrity put a very private painter at risk. The innocent joy on which her art rested might have been further threatened by formal training. At 21, Peggy finally entered the Royal Academy Schools; but, the year being 1939, she soon switched to the

Women's Land Army. Perhaps the transfer was a blessing for the artist continued to portray, in a brilliantly idiosyncratic way, the details of her life in the country – the joy of family ties and nature's abundance – that lay closest to her heart.

Her horizons and her art were broadened by travel, with early visits to Belgium and Holland; but France was to provide the greatest inspiration. After the war she made prolonged trips across the Channel, especially to Cézanne country in Provence, where the warm, bright and vibrant colours of the landscape and its greatest artists came to dominate her once soft and subtle palette. In later paintings, the gentle contours and cool, clear light of Suffolk were imbued with harmonic hues of a Mediterranean intensity while the front at Aldeburgh became as gay as Trouville. Such tints pleased the Fauvist-influenced Matthew Smith, who bought one of Peggy's pictures in 1951.

While living, from 1946, with her brother's family at Newbourn, near Ipswich, she still exhibited widely, but her name had lost its youthful novelty. In 1960 she moved to Westleton, an isolated village between Aldeburgh and Southwold, and in 1964 to nearby Middleton, first caring for her elderly mother and then waging her own battle against cancer. Even

Peggy Somerville *Summer, Aldeburgh,* oil on panel, 46 × 78cm.

Peggy Somerville *Sunshades,*
Aldeburgh, **c. 1965, oil on canvas,**
39 × 62cm.

in the darkening days before her death, at the age of 57, her vigorous oils, watercolours and especially pastels were touched by scarcely a shadow. The simplest motif was made magical, as mosaics of colour floated towards abstraction. Although appearing, like Gwen John, to retreat from the outside world, Peggy Somerville poured a rich interior life – rare sensuality and sensitivity – into beautiful paintings. And if a certain yielding quality had given way to robust design, remarkable serenity remained.

LIKE Peter Coker, **Keith Grant** (b. Liverpool, 1930) is a contemporary painter in the English Romantic landscape tradition of Constable and Turner. Both delight in the changing effects of light and weather. Both are drawn to extremes.

Keith Grant *Spindrift I,* 1986,
acrylic and watercolour on
board, 50 × 62cm.

From his home in Sussex, Grant travels to record fantastic rock and ice formations of the Far North, the jungles of French Guiana and the arid splendour of Israel's Negev Desert. The Royal College of Art graduate finds material for pictures on sea journeys, and his love of elemental shorelines has also brought him to watch the waves at Aldeburgh. His work is always expressive, dramatic and painterly, and he is preoccupied with the psychological significances of natural forms.

Symbolism is enhanced in his particular brand of refined simplification and abstraction, though the subject is never obscured. He has executed memorials to Benjamin Britten; and his striking Aldeburgh painting *Spindrift* – spray blown along the surface of the sea – is another elegy. Keith Grant's work may also be seen as a tribute to nature and a manifesto on the need for urgent action to protect threatened environments.

A Fresher Gale Ipswich to Framlingham

A fresher gale
Begins to wave the woods
    and stir the streams,
Sweeping with shadowy gusts
    the fields of corn.

These lines from John Thomson's poem, *Summer*, were quoted by Constable in a letter of April 1826 to Archdeacon Fisher of Salisbury, in which he explained the mood of his newly-painted picture, *The Cornfield*.

George Rushton *Tuddenham,*
c. 1925, watercolour, 40 × 57cm.

The fame of the nineteenth-century artists grouped around Cotman and Crome in Norwich cast a long shadow, perhaps unfairly putting the neighbouring Suffolk School in the shade. But, between the death of Constable and the birth of Munnings, the county at the heart of East Anglia boasted some powerful landscape painters – among them Thomas Churchyard and the brothers Thomas and E. R. Smythe. Similarly, the School of Art at Ipswich has had a record of achievement to rival that of its more celebrated counterpart in Norwich.

Between 1906 and 1929, the principal at the School of Art was **George Rushton** (1868-1948), who was also elected a member of both the Royal Institute of Painters in Water-colours and the Royal Society of British Artists, and who had a genius for discovering and developing creativity in others. On a trawl of

local schools, he spotted some drawings by **Leonard Squirrell** (1893-1979). Soon the youngster was at the Ipswich School of Art (along with another later noted local landscapist, Albert Ribbans), embarking on a career as one of the region's greatest watercolourists. Many have perceived the influence of John Sell Cotman in Squirrell's orderly painting; but crisp design and a brilliant use of colour patches also echo work by Rushton, who for some time had practised the art of stained glass.

Leonard Squirrell, born in Ipswich, was painfully shy all his life. His natural reserve was deepened by slight deafness and a speech impediment, which, linked to a shaking nervous affliction, could leave him at first meetings able to utter barely a word. But his hand rarely faltered. And he was both agile and strong-nerved in his determination to absorb

the atmosphere of his native town. 'When out of school, my whole time was occupied by outdoor sketching', the artist recalled towards the end of his life. 'I haunted the docks which in those days were filled with full-rigged sailing ships. The granaries and maltings in Fore Street with their piles of sacks and dusty rafters provided many a subject and trained my hand to draw. I emphasise that because, as mainly a topographical artist, good drawing has been the aim and substance of my whole career.' At 18, he executed in pen and watercolour a view of Ipswich and the River Orwell from the top of the town's gasometer, which entailed several daring climbs on an external spider ladder. The work (retained by Rushton and now in the Ipswich collection) was among a series of drawings which won its maker a gold medal in a national art schools competition.

Squirrell was now gaining attention. He first exhibited at the Royal Academy – where later he would show in an unbroken sequence of 47 years – at the age of 17; and, after Ipswich, went on to study at the Slade. Besides a facility in pencil and watercolour, the young artist was also emerging as a skilful etcher: in 1915 he took the British Institution Scholarship in Engraving.

Although he worked in Yorkshire, Scotland, Italy and France, Squirrell was happiest in East Anglia – and especially in Suffolk. As he acquired a wife and family, he moved within Ipswich, then to Chippenhall Green, near Fressingfield, and finally to the village of Witnesham, close to his home town. The artist painted Woodbridge waterfront, Framlingham Castle, now-gone post mills at Wrentham and churches everywhere. But he had a special feeling for the intimacy of domestic architecture, and thus delighted in Suffolk's wealth of white- and pink-washed farms, and ancient village streets (such as Kersey, near Hadleigh). In the age of the bulldozer, Squirrell was also attracted to ruins. Indeed, his diploma work for the Royal Society of Painters in Water-colours – of which he was elected a member in 1941 – depicts a gaunt Tudor shell with the title *The Last Phase: Demolition at Stoke Street, Ipswich.* Such pictures were matter-of-fact records whose concerns were with tone, colour, composition and perspective. An apparent hardness here, in an otherwise sensitive man, baffled one friend, the Suffolk painter Fred Baldwin, who said: 'I don't think Len had any real feelings of sentiment for old buildings. They were just subjects. I remember how he laughed when some

Leonard Squirrell *The Port of Ipswich from the Big Gas Holder,* **1938, pencil and watercolour, 30 × 49cm.**

old houses in Ipswich had been pulled down just before we had gone to sketch them – fine old timber framed buildings and in place an advertisement hoarding had been put up. It made me sad but I think Len had already made a drawing of them so it didn't affect him. That was an attitude I could never quite understand.'

But, freed from sentimentality, he displayed a strength of artistic purpose that won comparison with his hero, John Sell Cotman. As Frank Short, president of the Royal Society of Painter-Etchers, wrote in the catalogue of a 1934 exhibition at London's Brook Street Gallery: 'Squirrell follows the tradition of the Norwich School and takes a high place in the art engendered by that tradition.' If he was a tributary, he was a substantial one. William Russell Flint captured the exact qualities of his work in the foreword for Squirrell's show at the New Gallery, Ipswich, in 1967. 'It has the desirable qualities of the best traditional watercolours,' he wrote, 'draughtsmanship, technique, clean and harmonious colour, balanced composition and serenity – in short, a reflection of the artist himself, a steadfast man and true.'

At first Squirrell painted out of doors, but later he preferred to make only pencil sketches from life, with a letter code for colour and tone. These would then be redrawn in enlarged form in the studio. Paint might be added to a sparse pencil structure, but usually a detailed drawing preceded the washes. Fred Baldwin recalled that Squirrell would stretch the paper and then, always working on a dry surface with a 'fairly large round pointed brush with a lot of water', would start on the sky. Observing the 'mess' of his friend's working methods, Baldwin 'could never understand how the result could look so beautifully clear and transparent. He never relied on the happy accident of masking and scratching out . . . as with a master, it all looked so deceptively easy.' The artist enjoyed working in pastel, which he used for drawing rather than rubbed to give a smooth surface, but finally abandoned the medium as he could find no satisfactory fixative.

Leonard Squirrell *Our Town in 1933*, pen, ink and watercolour, 34 × 50cm.

He had a workmanlike approach to his art, in part born out of necessity. Once, when asked whether he had to wait for 'inspiration', he replied that it was a luxury he could not afford. Endeavouring to support a family in a notoriously precarious field, he had to be both swift and flexible. Like Rowland Hilder – whose choice of subject and handling of paint also bears comparison with Squirrell – the artist burned the midnight oil on motley commissions: book jackets and illustrations, calendars, greetings cards, postcards, paintings for businesses and marvellous railway prints and posters. Each spring and autumn he sent a picture to the Royal Watercolour Society in London, and for 64 consecutive years showed in annual exhibitions of the Ipswich Art Club, of which he was a linchpin (and which organised a major retrospective display of his work at Ipswich's Christchurch Mansion, in 1978, the year before his death).

Leonard Squirrell's life was touched by tragedy: his son, Martin, died of cancer at the age of 24. As art editor of the *East Anglian Magazine*, the young man had proved an impressive illustrator – some said that, with time, he might have outshone his father. But Leonard, though grieving, remained the true professional: almost at once he helped to fill the editorial gap left by his son's death. Work was always a solace.

Heading north-east from Ipswich, the visitor may be lured by the timeless charms of Woodbridge and Wickham Market. But between these picture postcard towns on the River Deben lies hidden the scattered village of Dallinghoo. It comprises a curve of council houses; ancient farms and cottages, some overrun by bind-weed and once-neat hedges, others

I LLNESS IS A curious but not infrequent ally for an artist, and **Walter Daniel Batley** (1850-1936) was a beneficiary of smallpox. As an ailing child he was moved from Ipswich to a cottage brushed by invigorating sea breezes at Felixstowe. Here, confined for long periods, he could do little but draw and paint. By the age of 19 he had found his health, his talent and a determination to devote himself to art. At the Ipswich School of Art his near contemporaries were Frederick George Cotman and the Yoxford-born portraitist William Robert Symonds. Following Cotman to London, he won the South Kensington competition gold medal for figure drawing in 1874, around the time he entered the Royal Academy Schools. That same year saw the foundation of the Ipswich Fine Art Club (later the Ipswich Art Club), of which Batley remained, for 60 years, a luminary. In successive waves, the society also attracted such diverse talents as Anna Airy, Leonard Squirrell, Edward Seago and Cor Visser.

Walter Batley *On the Road, Rushmere*, 1923, oil on canvas, 102 × 128cm.

Like many late Victorian painters, Walter Batley depicted the dramatic scenery of Switzerland, Yorkshire, Derbyshire and Cornwall on holiday expeditions. But Suffolk was his true canvas, and his captivation was complete when he married the daughter of an Ipswich house decorator, in 1878. Local heathlands and tree-lined lanes, and the coast from Southwold to Bawdsey, were favourite haunts. Experiments with narrative pictures had true-to-life backdrops: *His First Vote,* an 1884 study of an elderly farm labourer, newly-enfranchised by the Third Reform Act, was set in the village of Tuddenham.

In 1889 the Batleys and their five children moved from Ipswich to Rushmere St Andrew, to a Georgian farmhouse beside a winding country lane bordered by elms, hedges, ponds and low barns. Here was an endlessly changing scene of which the artist never tired. His resulting pictures were popular until the late 1880s, when sales at the Ipswich Fine Art Club and acceptances at the Royal Academy began to decline. Batley's atmospheric work, freely painted and with feeling for the effects of light, was in sympathy with the emergent New English Art Club of Wilson Steer, whom he may have met at Walberswick. His oil *On The Road,* painted after a move back to Felixstowe, was rejected by the Royal Academy in 1924. The following year it was hung at the Paris Salon.

Batley came full circle in 1928 when he and his wife returned to Ipswich, to live at The Anchorage, in Cauldwell Hall Road. The untamed heathlands of Martlesham and Foxhall were then within walking distance of his doorstep.

Leonard Squirrell *Kersey,* **1928, pastel, 40 × 40cm.**

in stages of gentrification; a Georgian manor and a church, with a Victorian lych-gate wrecked by the great gale of October 1987. For 20 years this tranquil hamlet was home to the watercolourist **David Evans** (1929-88), a similarly quiet man, whose art was nevertheless at times driven by a whirlwind.

Beyond the summer gardens bright with bedding plants, cosy with the occasional gnome or plastic heron, stands a lone farmhouse, significantly turned away from the road. Rural isolation and a cheap asking price made Potash Farm ideal for a painter who, in 1969, sought to escape from London. At once

David Evans *Potash Farm Garden,*
c. 1979, watercolour.

David Evans and his partner set about taming the two-acre site, to secure a dream of self-sufficiency. Chickens were purchased, herbs and vegetables planted. They grew soft fruit and sweet corn, and, in fine summers, picked figs from a majestic tree. Wheat was sown and flour ground. Greenhouses held peppers and tomatoes. Soon part of an adjoining field was rotavated for more potatoes, marrows and pumpkins. After every harvest, bunches of onions and garlic were hung on a barn wall to dry in the sun.

This plot of Suffolk soil, complete with flowers bursting from borders and honeysuckle pouring over disused pig pens, also enabled the artist to bloom. Raised a suburban Londoner, Evans trained at the Central School, Holborn, under Keith Vaughan. As a young sophisticate he exhibited modish photomontages and designed a mural for a Knightsbridge soup kitchen, before tiring of city fashion. Experiments in watercolour coincided with the move to East Anglia.

Establishing a simple and domestic life in the country, he allowed his creativity free rein. Early daffodils, window-sill geraniums, prize vegetables, Rhode Island reds scratching in the yard – natural inspiration was all around. He looked at things, then looked deeper to uncover the unexpected. Behind high hedges he found a car dump with a crane crunching dead metal, and from this unprepossessing scene created a glorious painting which he titled *Field of Cloth of Tin.*

The artist also looked further, to life in the barely undulating Suffolk fields that seemed to recede into a kind of infinity beyond his own hedge. Moreover, he had a remarkably rich visual imagination and memory so that, from his rural retreat, he was able to conjure up caustically witty comments on modern urban life, and to conduct motley grand performances – in effect to deliver devastating punchlines – on giant sheets of paper. The bull-fight crowds, ritual bathers in the River Ganges and concert audiences of his paintings peopled his secluded world.

He fretted over supplies of the right size and quality of paper, confiding to his diary in 1972: 'I am uncomfortable "working" on a sheet smaller than 40 inches by 27 inches. I would like to do bigger ones <u>but</u>, alas, it is nigh impossible to buy larger good paper and awkward, to say the least, to cart or handle cardboard larger than this. It is nothing to do with "one's emotional content fitting the right-sized envelope": it is merely practical. My early horrors were small since I only had a drawing board this size, lived in pokey rooms with little light and was always on the move. Also the storing of the work: The largest folio to be bought is still too small.'

Evans found the low, flattish Suffolk landscape perfect for painting. In his tiny studio, overlooking his vegetable garden, he could work in the late afternoon, without shadows intruding. He worked quickly, with little pencil preparation on the surface of the paper but after copious notes and sketches. Errors were turned into advantages; only rarely was a painting abandoned. When asked how he controlled the notoriously tricky medium of watercolour over pictures of such unusual size and scale, he replied: 'I use bigger brushes to put on a bigger area of wash. Some of the brushes are almost up to the sizes used in household painting.'

In his studio, flanked by cases of brilliant butterflies and an antique screen caging birds of paradise, he worked against a background of music. As a

child, Evans had been torn between composing and painting; but, after a juvenile score sent to Benjamin Britten drew no encouragement, he settled on art. Or rather, he slowly became a symphonic colourist – and in his notebooks each painting was always referred to as a numbered 'opus'.

Danger stalks in many of Evans's pictures. Overgrown foliage appears voracious, predatory. The towering herbaceous borders of certain paintings appear as if viewed by insects or shrews: the sinister greenery may contain killer plants, or at any moment the claw of a prowling cat, lurking unseen behind bloated leaves, may burst through the canvas.

The work of David Evans has been compared with that of Edward Burra. Both liked outsized watercolours; their sights soared over strange vistas and social situations they had seen, remembered or imagined; macabre images, dark humour and an undercurrent of menace flowed through both channels. But the poetry of the best Evans paintings remains unique. His lyrical vision was deeply felt – as he wrote in his diary: 'Most of the time we are offered by artists only what they have partly digested or more

David Evans, photographed in his studio in 1980 and his painting *The Allotment*, 1986, watercolour, 74 × 117cm.

often than not what they are still chewing in their mouths . . . I don't think anyone produces anything of value until it has actually got into the bloodstream . . .'

But what caused the underlying sense of unease? Evans knew that nature was indeed red in tooth and claw. His work also hints at the disturbance that other people can bring, and at inner tensions linked to sexuality. Other pressures intruded. The artist could never live on the proceeds of sales: he worked in a

David Evans *Gladioli*, 1987, watercolour, 88 × 61cm (below) and *Daffodils*, 1987, watercolour, 93 × 63cm (right).

mushroom factory, until made redundant. Then he found a position as a part-time porter at St Audrey's Hospital, Melton – a psychiatric unit within cycling distance of his home. This acted as a sort of deliverance. He adored hard physical labour and, best of all, portering left his mind free to mull over the sight of people expressing the vividly varied reality that mental illness may intensify. Some studies are almost hallucinatory. Images of souls in bafflement or turmoil occur repeatedly; but however crowded and insane the scene, each figure plays out an individual drama. While aware of the human comedy, this creative spirit remained compassionate.

In Suffolk, as he found his artistic voice and developed a new spiritual awareness, he gradually relaxed – until, towards the end, after recovering from a major operation, he achieved what some might call a state of grace. As his tensions eased and his technique became more assured, his landscapes became more gentle, ever more vast, and inhabited by fewer and fewer figures.

Over New Year 1988, David Evans had been working on a painting of a major road cutting a course through rural East Anglia, but had discarded it when realising that the traffic he had painted was travelling in the wrong direction. Early one morning, a few weeks later, while attempting to cross the A12 on his way to work, he was killed when his bicycle collided with a van.

AFTER GAINSBOROUGH   Hadleigh to Bury St Edmunds

On the outskirts of the ribbon town of Hadleigh in south Suffolk, overlooking the valley of the River Brett, stands a buttressed and gabled house dating from the sixteenth century. Benton End was home to the painter and plantsman **Cedric Morris** (1889-1982) for the last 42 years of his life. Here he produced a famous garden and down-to-earth oils of people, birds, flowers, vegetables and surrounding landscapes. Here, too, with Arthur Lett-Haines, he ran the East Anglian School of Painting and Drawing.

Morris is said to have met the twice-married 'Lett' on Armistice Night, 1918; they remained together, despite a chasm between their characters,

until the latter's death, in 1978. With a cosmopolitan curiosity, Haines tried out many modernist ideas in his painting and sculpture. But essentially, he sacrificed his own career to promote his partner and ensure the smooth running of their household and art school. Morris had explored abstraction and surrealism during early periods in Cornwall, Paris and London, and had been a leading member of the avant-garde Seven and Five Society. His shows in the capital had been huge successes. But by 1930, tiring of technical experiments and rebelling against the commercial art system, he moved to Suffolk. In the country he held fast to a direct style, with his eyes

Cedric Morris *Landscape of Shame*, c. 1960, oil on canvas, 75 × 100cm.

fixed firmly on a subject. He became an outsider in every sense, pursuing a personal vision within a self-contained circle of students and admirers. And the plump vegetables produced by his labour of love in the garden were prepared by Haines into celebrated meals.

On abandoning London, they moved first to The Pound – a farmhouse outside Higham, four miles from Hadleigh, where Morris could indulge his passion for birds and plants. As he tamed the nettle-ridden garden, his audience often consisted of a peacock, cockatoo, mackaw, Muscovy ducks and mallard. Meanwhile, artist friends worked indoors: visitors included Francis Hodgkins, Dora Carrington and Barbara Hepworth (whose first husband, the sculptor John Skeaping, was to stay for several

Cedric Morris *Layham Mill,* oil on canvas, 63 × 53cm.

months after the break-up of their marriage, adorning the garden with stone and marble torsos). A rural idyll mixing hard work and heady parties was established from the start.

In 1937 Haines and Morris began their art school in an old house in the centre of Dedham, across the border in Essex. After six months it had attracted almost 60 students and was staging its first exhibition. A way of life was being championed. As one prospectus ran: 'We want to . . . provide the student with a place where he can work in freedom with every opportunity and encouragement to find his particular form of expression and incidentally to give him the opportunity of creating the atmosphere of enthusiasm and enjoyment which we feel is essential to the development of his perceptions and the production of good work.' Age was no barrier. One of the school's longest serving students was Ipswich-born, Slade-trained Lucy Harwood, who produced vividly coloured landscapes of the scenes around Upper Layham, where she lived from 1940. But the most remarkable graduate was Lucian Freud, whose raw, nerve-exposed portraits have something in common with the 'shrieking likenesses' of Morris. His presence was literally burnt into the memory of the school. With fellow student David Carr, Freud had worked on late into one evening, during the summer of 1939. A discarded cigarette probably proved disastrous, for during the night the building was engulfed by fire. The next day Morris and his students painted the smouldering ruins. The search for new premises led to Benton End, which had lain empty for 15 years. Henceforward the tutors' home, school and lodgings for their students were to be on a single site.

A world both free and self-contained, as formed by the East Anglian School of Painting and Drawing, can be seen in Morris's pictures. He was largely self-taught as an artist. Born in South Wales and the descendant of a coal magnate whose baronetcy he would inherit in 1947, he did not begin to paint seriously until 1918. By that time he had worked on ranches in Canada, as a liftboy and dishwasher in New York, given up a course in singing at the Royal College of Music, and trained horses for the war (alongside his irascible future neighbour, Alfred Munnings). His mature work was concerned with bold pattern, texture and colour, underpinned by a powerful sense of place and atmosphere. Surface details were jettisoned in favour of capturing the inner life of the subject. Some unusually tender pictures sought to 'provoke a lively sympathy with the mood of birds which ornithological exactitude may tend to destroy'; a desert of feathered corpses, in *Landscape of Shame*, was dedicated to a pesticide manufacturer. His was the art of living dangerously – using stiff paint thickly, in short strokes, with no

THE ENDLESSLY varying textures of flint, brick and stone, merging in the sculptural surfaces of weathered walls, have inspired the etchings and engravings of **Valerie Thornton** (b. 1931). Farms and churches throughout her adopted East Anglia have proved favourite subjects.

A fellow of the Royal Society of Painter-Etchers and Engravers, Valerie Thornton trained in Paris under the great print-maker S. W. Hayter in the early 1950s, before setting up her own Surrey workshop. She first visited Benton End in 1956, with stained-glass artist Rosemary Rutherford who was formerly a student there; ten years later she moved to Colchester when her husband, Michael Chase, was appointed curator of The Minories. Haines and Morris became friends and influences.

Her work stands as a tribute to the architects, masons and labourers of East Anglia, whose only epitaph lies in the fabric of the grand and vernacular buildings they helped to create. It also attests to painstaking precision in an unyielding medium. 'In etching the artist works with a hard intractable material', John Rothenstein once observed. 'The open bite system, which Valerie has made very much her own, is capable of producing a relief of pits on the metal plate – pits

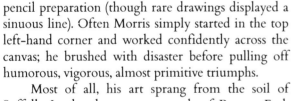

Valerie Thornton *Boxford*, 1974, etching, 39 × 62cm.

which hold the ink – producing very rich marks on the printed sheet – indeed in her hands the plate has an almost sculpted presence.

Rothenstein added: 'In the direct frontal view, chosen again and again, we sense that ancient walls, wrinkled and stained by the hazards of their history, find a clear mirror in these beautiful presentations.'

Based since 1974 in an ancient farmhouse at Chelsworth, Valerie Thornton and Michael Chase have travelled to France and Italy to record details of architecture and landscape in print or paint. But from the fruit of continued trips across East Anglia, the viewer can perceive the same spirit that guided the builders of our heritage.

pencil preparation (though rare drawings displayed a sinuous line). Often Morris simply started in the top left-hand corner and worked confidently across the canvas; he brushed with disaster before pulling off humorous, vigorous, almost primitive triumphs.

Most of all, his art sprang from the soil of Suffolk. In the three-acre grounds of Benton End, Morris replaced a sea of elderberry and bramble with old-fashioned roses, bulbous species and irises. Plants were begged from cottage gardens or collected during foreign travels, particularly to the Mediterranean. Still more were bred. New irises – including the first pure pink, a near black, seven ice-blues and a milky mauve – bore the prefix 'Benton'. Their colours, set against yellow-green stems, dominated the painter's palette. In so many canvases their towering forms are viewed as if by a gardener, on hands and knees, weeding around their roots. Still lifes of vegetables, too, were presented with the pride of a self-sufficient producer.

Cedric Morris died, aged 92, when the Tate Gallery was at last preparing a retrospective exhibition of his work. For seven years he had been unable to paint due to failing eyesight, the school had faded out and the garden was fast returning to wilderness. But his achievement was assured. Looking back down

the decades, Ronald Blythe has written: 'I always retain a composite Monet-like vision of Benton End

Cedric Morris *Stoke by Nayland Church,* 1940, oil on canvas, 60 × 81cm.

Cedric Morris *Blackbird*, 1953, oil on canvas, 92 × 116cm.

MAGGI HAMBLING was born in Sudbury in 1945, and brought up in Hadleigh. She studied at Benton End from the age of 15, and later trained at the Ipswich School of Art, and in London at Camberwell and the Slade. She has been noted for powerful portraits and sunrises, and a spell as the first artist in residence at the National Gallery. Lett Haines has remained her greatest mentor.

The artist visited Cedric Morris in Ipswich hospital on 6th and 7th February 1982. Returning to London, the following morning she made this drawing from memory. It was barely completed when word came that Morris had died.

on a summer's afternoon just before the tea bell, with students, roses, easels, cats, iris beds, labyrinthine paths, secretive walls and multifarious palettes all joined in a conspiracy of colour and light.'

Morris's belief that 'you can't really teach painting, but you can encourage talent' was a guiding principle of the Colchester Art Society, which he founded with John Nash and Rowland Suddaby in 1946. The grouping came to attract Edward Bawden,

Maggi Hambling *Cedric*, 1982, charcoal, 72 × 56cm.

SOMETIMES referred to as England's Berthe Morisot – after the long-overshadowed French Impressionist – **Elinor Bellingham Smith** (1906-88) painted with deftness and delicacy her impressions of the Suffolk landscape, following a move to Boxford in 1957. Her final years were spent at nearby Bildeston.

Forced by injury to abandon training as a ballet dancer, she went to the Slade as one of the last pupils of Tonks – and was one of the few female students to gain his respect. Friends and contemporaries included William Coldstream, Claude Rogers and Rodrigo Moynihan, whom she married in 1931 (a separation preceded her move to Suffolk). In such company, she absorbed what was to become the Euston Road School's emphasis on hard observation, but took the chill from a cold vision with a liveliness and a sensitivity all her own.

In Suffolk she produced almost winsome portraits of children in the countryside. Stronger were her cool winter landscapes, subtly toned in blues and greys, with rapid, often staccato brush strokes picking out rushes and bare branches from an otherwise pervading mist. Such scenes were presented like filigree work in iron. The critic David Sylvester likened her lithe script to dance of the hand 'not danced to give herself light entertainment but in an effort to find an equivalent on canvas for her experience of being alone in a flat country under a great canopy of sky which gives the illusion that it reflects the turbulence and the euphoria and the fears and the hopelessness and the releases that come and go in the mind.'

Elinor Bellingham Smith *Winter Afternoon*, 1952, oil on canvas, 51 × 61cm.

John Aldridge and Michael Rothenstein, as well as staff and students of the local art college – including John O'Connor – and many gifted amateurs; and it has continued to display remarkable dynamism in its exhibitions at The Minories. But the first phase, when selection committee meetings were contests between Morris and Suddaby, is rightly regarded as a high point.

JOHN O'CONNOR (b. 1913) head of Colchester School of Art and co-ordinator of art education in North Essex, 1948-64, is also an accomplished book illustrator, wood engraver and painter in oils and watercolour.

Trained at the Royal College of Art, O'Connor lived in the Brett Valley between 1961 and 1975 – first at Higham and then at Shelley. The atmosphere of the tranquil area inspired some fine autumnal pictures of river, foliage and fields.

Elected a senior fellow of the Royal Society of Painters in Water-colours in 1965, he now lives and works in Galloway.

John O'Connor *Suffolk Landscape*, c. 1960, oil on canvas, 76 × 61cm.

Like Morris, **Rowland Suddaby** (1912–72) was very conscious of his roots in industrial Britain – Yorkshire, in his case, where he had worked in a steel foundry. Both had struck up an early friendship with the painter Christopher Wood, and had been much influenced by his lyrical landscapes and semi-naive style. (Wood's untimely death – he was killed by a train at Salisbury station when aged 29 – was a major loss to British art.) And, having found striking success in London, both men met with relative obscurity after settling in Suffolk.

Suddaby has been described by the East Anglian painter Henry Collins as a 'live wire'. His gouache landscapes exude a nervous energy, their quick patterns, drawn directly with the brush, express joyful excitement at the sheer freshness of the world. 'They are intellectual and technical exercises on a theme provided by nature', wrote the critic Clive Bell in 1936. 'The artist has been thrilled by something he has seen and the purpose of the picture is to express

the moment of delight.' Soaring spirits are also suggested by a brilliant and daring use of colour, likened by more than one critic to that of Suddaby's hero, Matisse. However, many pictures rest on a firm structure of black, white and grey. It is not irrelevant that, having reached London after studies at the Sheffield College of Art, he ornamented the titles and produced cartoons for black and white films in Wardour Street.

The move to the capital proved rash. Suddaby told the *Hull Daily Mail,* in 1937: 'When I was 19 I sold one of my pictures to a Sheffield man for £15, and was so elated that I got married and went to London with the proceeds.' Unable to sell any more paintings, he walked the streets looking for work, often going hungry. At his lowest point he sold his entire studio of 50 pictures or more for £10 (the buyer later selling a quarter of them for £100). The film job was a godsend. He painted in his spare time, until establishing a reputation. Mixing with other

Rowland Suddaby *Willy Lott's Cottage,* **c. 1939, watercolour, 38 × 56cm.**

artists, he dabbled with abstraction but soon returned to the observable world. He travelled widely. Posters of 'British Landmarks' were executed for Shell. And, by the time leading galleries in London and overseas were queuing for exhibitions, the artist and his wife had taken a weekend house at Thorpe-le-Soken, in Essex. East Anglian scenes joined the nude and still lifes pouring from his studio.

Then war was declared and Suddaby, seeing children issued with gasmasks in a London playground, moved his family to Great Cornard, near Sudbury. Asthma and a weak heart limited his active service to the duties of an air-raid warden. He also depicted landscapes around his new home for the Government's 'Recording Britain' scheme, designed textiles (which would later feature in a number of paintings) and embarked on book illustration. His watercolours and ink drawings worked well in print,

particularly in Olive Cook's guide to Suffolk, part of the 'Vision of England' series published by Paul Elek.

The impact of the war brought a more sombre note into Suddaby's art. Traces of the Neo-Romantic movement appeared, with plaintive imagery of dark, stylised trees and vegetation. At the same time he was re-examining the work and subjects of Constable and Gainsborough. He painted Willy Lott's cottage at Flatford, facing the line of brooding trees that Constable had omitted. Other Suffolk and Essex landscapes, often with farms or churches as central motifs, shudder beneath blackening skies. They seem to be held in an air of tension and suspense. In 1946, the critic of *The Studio* noted an expression of 'the mystifying variations of English countryside between storms – these moods that seem to glower and grin at the same time.'

Rowland Suddaby continued to exhibit, but

Edward Middleditch *Cornfield*, 1978, chalk, 70 × 83cm (far left) and *Stubble Burning*, 1980, chalk, 51 × 64cm (left).

T HE PRAIRIE-LIKE fields of south Suffolk, now stripped of hedges, inspired lyrical late drawings by **Edward Middleditch** (1923-87). Dense stalks of corn merging into apparently empty expanses and the pattern of flames licking autumn stubble are presented in a straight-forward manner which only enhance their deeper mystery. Born in Chelmsford, the Royal Academician (elected 1973) lived for most of his last 25 years at Boxford, mid-way between Hadleigh and Sudbury. Close observation of landscape always shaped his art.

Training at the Royal College of Art from 1949, under Ruskin Spear and John Minton, Middleditch produced stark and memorable images from the start. They won him association with the 'Kitchen Sink School' of social realists, comprising his contemporaries John Bratby, Derrick Greaves and Jack Smith. Austerity, Cold War and a sense of the futility of the recent fighting – Middleditch had been severely wounded during the advance into Germany – lurked behind dour studies, set amid the wreckage of daily life. But Edward

Middleditch remained an artist apart. Messages or movements did not concern him. He was purely, as one critic put it, a 'poet of appearances'. Using chalk, charcoal, pen or brush, he combined an open vision with a sophisticated intelligence to set down what he saw. Flowers and spiky foliage became favourite subjects, always placed in the centre of the picture space – often larger than life, but never exaggerated for dramatic effect.

Middleditch was also a noted teacher. He served as head of fine art at the Norwich School of Art from 1964 to 1984, before becoming keeper of the Royal Academy, in charge of Schools. In Norwich his department was run on the belief that students should learn by seeing paintings, drawings and prints being made around them. Artists who worked under this studio system included Michael Andrews, Lucian Freud, Derrick Greaves, John Lessore, Colin Self, Philip Sutton and John Wonnacott – all, whether resident or visiting, substantial contributors to the strength of modern art in East Anglia.

Rowland Suddaby *Spout Farm, Great Cornard*, **pen, ink and wash, 38 × 56cm (above).**

increasingly sporadically, until 1967. After that, he concentrated on running the Gainsborough House museum and gallery in Sudbury. There has been a considerable revival of interest in his work since his death.

Above the Stour Valley, usually unnoticed in the wider landscape beloved of Suddaby and many other painters, stands the tiny hamlet of Hickbush. It comprises a clump of cottages and a farm at the end of a track, with a few fields rolling between breaks of trees and broken hedges towards Henny and Sudbury. Its gentle contours and seasonal changes have been concentrated into a number of remarkable pictures by Patrick George, who lived here from 1961 until 1984. Such intense contemplations of a single locality also express the essence of the English countryside.

The son of a Lancashire merchant turned Cotswold farmer, **Patrick George** (b. 1923) was a schoolboy when William Coldstream arrived to paint his English master, one W. H. Auden. After a period at the Edinburgh College of Art, and war service with the Royal Navy – during which he ranged from the Atlantic to the Far East, and emerged with ample supplies of awning for canvas – he was taught by Coldstream (as well as Claude Rogers, Victor Pasmore and Lawrence Gowing) at Camberwell.

A LARGE part of the painted world of **Reginald Brill** (1902-74) revolved around the rural life of Suffolk – especially Lavenham, which he knew from the early 1930s. His compelling portraits, figure compositions, landscapes and still lifes have a deceptive simplicity.

Here was no untutored primitive. Though largely unschooled during childhood years in London and Yorkshire, he later attended evening classes at St Martin's School of Art and won a scholarship to the Slade in 1921. Awarded the Prix de Rome in decorative painting in 1927, he studied in Italy at the British School of Rome, before returning to teach in London. His headship of the Kingston School of Art, 1934-62, was a great success.

Introduced to Lavenham by an early patron, Colonel Gayer-Anderson, he fell in love with the village of medieval beauty built on wool wealth. After the Gayer-Anderson brothers bequeathed their Tudor home, The Little Hall, as a hostel for art students, Brill and his wife became wardens. Today the house is the headquarters of the Suffolk Preservation Society.

From his studio in the chapel of the Guildhall, Reginald Brill travelled to Sudbury, Bury St Edmunds, and even to King's Lynn, to draw

Reginald Brill *Guildhall, Lavenham*, 1968, pen and wash.

livestock auctions. He adored village fêtes and shows, depicted ancient streets and market squares clustered with people, or a lonely figure in the waiting room of Lavenham station (wound down in the 1960s). Although he idolised the painter William Roberts, he was also influenced by Stanley Spencer – notably in one picture of a nativity scene set in a barn in Cockfield.

Patrick George *The Opposite Bank*, 1983, oil on canvas, 84 × 213cm.

Long before he joined the staff at the Slade, where he was to teach with distinction for almost 40 years (ending as Slade Professor, 1985-87), the painter shared his own tutors' belief in objective observation. But his drawn-from-life portraits and industrial landscapes would prove both precise and poetic.

For Patrick George, painting is a slow and painstaking process. The first of the Hickbush pictures, *Wooded Landscape,* was begun in the summer of 1961

and continued each July for the following five years. Perennial problems of painting out of doors, worsened by East Anglia's fickle weather, forced him to revise his plan of action. Although some later oils carry the haze of high summer, others display a pared down seasonal amalgam, with trees both bare and laden and the earth turning in receding folds green or golden with corn, stubbled cream, then ploughed a grey-brown and gradually bleached lighter by wind

Patrick George *Valley Farm,* **1982, oil on canvas, 102 × 112cm.**

and rain. Here a small patch of Suffolk landscape is presented in all its annual guises.

All his landscape painting is executed in the afternoon, throughout the year. Exposed on a hillside, he anchors his easel with blocks of wood or guy-ropes, takes up his brushes, pencil and compass and settles into the scene. Birds, hares, even weasels wander past. But he is not lost in some romantic reverie. Like Constable, he paints industrial places – his pictures are appreciations of 'good husbandry'. He often centres a view on stark farm buildings, while electricity pylons, swooping and striding across successive canvases, socket each subject into a broader grid.

Although Patrick George now lives at Great Saxham, near Bury St Edmunds, his routine is unchanged. When not working on portraits in London, he continues to be absorbed by what happens to a few score acres of Suffolk soil. For Lawrence Gowing: 'The informality and naturalness with which Patrick George shows the breadth and richness of a place, in images that have a splendid openness, have not often been paralleled in painting. His experiments in the ways that the real can carry its actual existence into painting with its delicate life intact, are difficult to forget – impossible, in fact, when you find yourself in rolling farmland in the late afternoon.'

Leaving Great Saxham, and meandering towards Haverhill, a network of country lanes may take the traveller to Little Thurlow. Here **Elisabeth Frink** (b. 1930) spent happy childhood years. Although she has lived subsequently in London, France and Dorset, she retains strong roots in south Suffolk. As a child home from boarding school, she watched the wildlife which would be used later as vehicles for sculpture and drawings. During the war she also shot hares, rabbits and pigeons to supplement the family's rations.

War-time East Anglia, still more than today, was dotted with airfields and army camps. The young Elisabeth Frink, whose father commanded a cavalry regiment, was deeply impressed by the military presence. She has vivid memories of crippled bombers limping back to nearby bases, or occasionally crashing into the fields around her home. The angular forms of some of her bird sculptures from the 1950s have been likened to the jagged fuselage of crashed planes. At the same time a number of spinning men appeared in her work, clad in flying gear, falling helplessly, out of control. Helmeted and goggled heads, inspired by pilots seen on Suffolk aerodromes, were to become a major element of her work.

Frink has used animal figures, but more often the head of a man, to express aggression and alienation. Her goggled heads evolved into anonymous oppressors. Then, in the 1970s, she saluted the victims

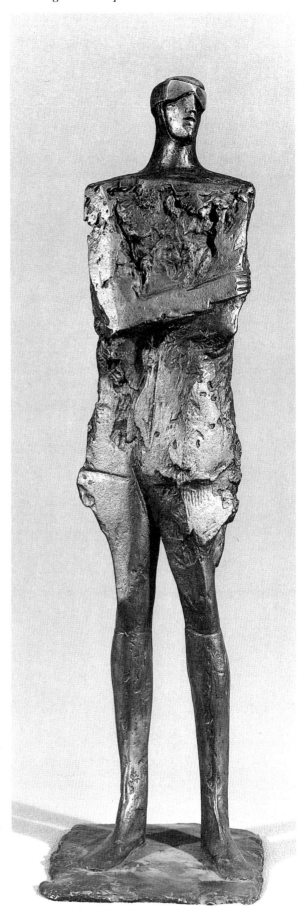

Elisabeth Frink *Helmeted Man*, **1968, bronze, 68cm high.**

Lionel Edwards *Newmarket*, 1938, watercolour and gouache, 48 × 73cm (right) and *Warren Hill*, 1932, oil on canvas, 50 × 74cm (below) – the artist considered this to be one of his best paintings.

of repression, creating a series of heroic heads, with faces masked in suffering (also a full-length figure of St Edmund, for Bury St Edmunds). She has won numerous public commissions and wide recognition, becoming a Royal Academician in 1977 and a Dame of the British Empire in 1982. Lately her work has seemed more tranquil, with figures of horsemen and naked athletes depicting an ideal man: calm, compassionate and striving for his fullest potential.

Elisabeth Frink's images of horses may have been inspired by the wild animals of the Camargue, rather than the racing world of Newmarket, which stretched beyond her childhood home. But the courses, sales and stables of the Suffolk town have attracted a string of equestrian painters down the centuries.

George Stubbs depicted the rubbing-down house on the heath; his successor as England's leading sporting painter, Ben Marshall, lived locally for 13 years from 1812. But some of the most memorable images of racing excitement in East Anglia have been captured by **Alfred Munnings.**

A regular visitor to Newmarket, Munnings maintained a studio here in the 1950s. His favourite subject showed horses and jockeys lined up at the starting point, raring to be off. One such picture smashed the auction record for the artist, when it was sold by Sotheby's of New York in 1987. Entitled *The Start At Newmarket: Study No. 4*, the elongated oil fetched a hammer price of $1.1 million.

Another familiar figure around Newmarket – and a comrade of Munnings in the Army Remount Service during the First World War – was **Lionel Edwards** (1878-1966). Based mostly in Hampshire, he travelled the country to record horses and riders in a variety of landscapes. 'First and foremost a fox-hunting man,' ran his obituary in *The Times,* 'he drew and painted what he loved doing and his remarkable eye for country was that of a man who sees the landscape from the saddle.' He was still riding to hounds in his eighties.

With a preference for gouache and watercolour, the artist liked to work outdoors whatever the weather. He began with a few pencil notes, then painted what John Betjeman immortalised in a typically bitter-sweet poem as 'a Lionel Edwards sky'. This would be followed by the landscape, and finally the horses and mounts. Detailed drawings were used for oils which were worked up later – amid frequent losses of confidence – in his studio. He wrote of another painter of horses, G. D. Armour: 'It rains and blows and men and horses get covered in mud in his pictures exactly as they do in the real thing.' Such a tribute could apply to Edwards himself.

Alfred Munnings *The Start at Newmarket, Study No. 4,* **oil on board, 93 × 183cm.**

The River Stour winds through one of the most unmarred valleys in East Anglia, which still clings to the title of Constable country. Roads and fields have been widened since John Constable painted here in the early 1800s, but strenuous conservation has preserved many of the ancient buildings and the spirit of a landscape charted by the master artist. The towers and pinnacles of parish churches at Dedham, Stratford St Mary and Stoke by Nayland remain as imposing features on an otherwise open skyline.

Like Constable, East Anglia's most famous painter of this century was the son of a miller. **Alfred James Munnings** (1878-1959) grew up at Mendham Mill, on the Norfolk-Suffolk border. The scenery of Waveney was his earliest love, but he also visited the Stour Valley with his father, who came from Stoke by Nayland. 'We found it beautiful,' he said of one trip, recalled in later life, 'unspoilt as in the days of Constable.' In 1920 he moved with his second wife to Dedham to live in Castle House, a fine Georgian building in a Tudor courtyard, looking out across paddocks and meadows.

After attending Redenhall Grammar School and Framlingham College, Munnings left Mendham at the age of 14 to train as a poster designer in Norwich. Each evening he would study at the Norwich School of Art, mostly under the guidance of the floral watercolourist Gertrude Offord. He also exhibited with the Norwich Art Circle; and the first of his 289 pictures to be hung by the Royal Academy was accepted for the summer exhibition of 1898. After a six-year apprenticeship he returned to his native village, to set up a studio in a carpenter's shop.

During the heyday of Edwardian England, Munnings worked hard 'trying to see colour' – using bold pigment in compositions of great originality. There were brief studies in Paris, followed by a still briefer summer stay at Frank Calderon's school for animal and landscape painting, at Finchingfield, Essex; and in 1904 he moved to Church Farm,

Alfred Munnings *Horse Sale*, 1902, pencil and watercolour, 27 × 42cm.

Swainsthorpe, five miles south of Norwich. With a straggle of horses, ponies and a donkey, a blue caravan and a cart for his canvases, Bob his handyman and a young runaway named Shrimp, Munnings went on long painting expeditions to the Ringland Hills and Costessey, and to Hoxne on the Waveney. He was also drawn to Cornwall, to a community of artists around Newlyn, founded by Stanhope Forbes and including Lamorna Birch, Charles Simpson, Harold Harvey and Laura Knight. With these kindred souls, Munnings explored a personal vision through a palette of Post-Impressionistic intensity. Astonishingly, he seemed unhindered by a disaster that had befallen him at the age of 20. Walking at Mulbarton, near Norwich, the young painter had collided with a briar while lifting a puppy over a thorn fence. The accident left him blinded in one eye.

But it is as a sublime portraitist of horses that Munnings is best known. Early in 1918 he was sent to France as an official war artist attached to the Canadian Cavalry Brigade, and to the end of his days he remained an enraptured recorder of sales, fairs hunts and races. In *An Artist's Life,* the first volume of a vivid autobiography, he savoured the memory of his first visit to the horse fair at Lavenham: 'What a sight! This famous fair of heavy draught-horses eclipsed anything of its kind I had ever seen.' And with great relish he also depicted the people whose lives revolved around ponies, shires and racing thorough-breds – the bowler-hatted buyers of heavy horses for company vans and brewers' drays in London, stable-boys, jockeys, farmhands, gypsies. His horse-centred scenes say a great deal about the multi-layered East Anglian society of his day.

Once installed at Dedham, Munnings worked in the grounds of his expensive home, using the studio he had transported from Swainsthorpe or a redundant open-topped omnibus facing a field of his beloved horses. He found both fame and notoriety. In 1928 a retrospective exhibition of his work at the Norwich Castle Museum attracted 86,000 visitors in six weeks. But, while longing to be free to paint East Anglian scenes – 'When you want peace, paint willows and lily-leaves', he wrote to his wife – the artist had to accept countless commissions for equestrian portraits in order to pay his bills. In 1944 he was elected president of the Royal Academy and was knighted. He took full advantage of his elevated status to fulminate against modern art – agreeing with Winston Churchill that the punishment he would like to mete out to Picasso would be to kick his backside. Not surprisingly, this complex and rumbustious man became caricatured as a blimpish bigot. The poetry and inventiveness of his best work was obscured. More than 30 years after the artist's death, his popularity at the salerooms climbs steadily, but his critical standing dawdles.

In 1986 a major loan exhibition opened in Manchester but failed to find exhibition space in London. Yet, as Nicholas Usherwood's introduction observed: 'Munnings is a painter of the English landscape scene of lyrical quality and historical importance.' Like Constable, he could capture the truth of a working landscape, with a technique

---

THE MENTOR of Edward Seago, **Bertram Priestman** (1868-1951) was also an enthusiastic recorder of East Anglian landscapes. For much of his adult life the Royal Academician (elected 1923) made annual painting tours of the region, often renting country houses in the area of his searches.

Having studied at the Slade, the Yorkshire-born artist exhibited at the Royal Academy from 1890 and became a member of the New English Art Club in 1896. Between portrait-painting spells in London, he travelled – to the Continent, but more often towards East Anglia. There were tours around the Great Dunmow and Felsted areas of Essex, and throughout Suffolk, where he had bases at Walberswick (notably 1914-15 and 1919-27), then Snape Hall and later still at Woodbridge. For many years he could be seen chugging along the country lanes in an old 1908 De Dion Bouton car, seeking out fresh subjects for his broadly handled oil paints.

At first Bertram Priestman depicted cattle in shaded pasture, evening scenes or low-toned seascapes. Over time his palette lightened as his eyes took in every nuance of green to be found in an East Anglian summer.

Bertram Priestman *Dedham from the Talbooth*, 1918, oil on canvas, 132 × 163cm.

Alfred Munnings *Haymaking on the Stour,* **oil on canvas, 50 × 60cm.**

embracing both delicacy and gusto. To his friend Laura Knight he was 'several people in one; for a flash a poet, a supersensitive creature of refined tastes and instincts, of culture; one moment canny, the next plunged back into great generosity and lavish extravagance.' These qualities flooded through his art.

In stark contrast to the formal grandeur of Castle House is a timber, brick and plaster farmhouse standing further along the Stour at Wormingford. Hidden in a hollow, and approached via a perilously rutted track, the low building of Bottengoms has settled into its surroundings, seemingly untouched by the centuries. A still air hangs about the place – recalling a painting by the countryman, gardener and landscape artist **John Nash** (1893-1977), who lived here from 1944.

When John and Christine Nash first arrived, there was no electricity and water was drawn from a stream running in an open culvert across the kitchen floor. During hot weather, milk and butter were cooled in a little waterfall near the door. Gradually, as paintings sold and commissions for book illustrations flowed, the house was made slightly more comfortable: the stream – supplying water for Bottengoms to this day – was diverted into the garden. But essentially, domestic conditions remained unchanged, being, as Ronald Blythe notes, 'less the result of poverty than of John and Christine's passion for things as they were. The past had everything to do with standards and little to do with nostalgia, and this included the warm, lamp-lit interiors and the crammed, luxuriant garden full of true cottage plants.

Alfred Munnings *Sunny June*, **1901, oil on canvas, 76 × 128cm.**

They possessed a stylishness and a simplicity of which they were quite unaware.'

In time the house was approached through an orchard of quinces, plums and greengages, fronting a neatly ordered plot of fruit and vegetables. Elsewhere, near enamel sinks of alpines and succulents, herbaceous beds and old-fashioned roses grew in romantic profusion; a series of ponds became fringed with

T HE FRENCH IMPRESSIONIST painter Camille Pissarro took his family to London in 1870, to escape the Franco-Prussian War. His eldest son, Lucien, made further visits during the 1880s, before finally settling in England in 1890. He became a naturalised Briton in 1916.

Lucien Pissarro (1863-1944) studied painting under his father, and was influenced by Seurat. In turn a member of the New English Art Club, Walter Sickert's Fitzroy Street and Camden Town groups, and the Society of Wood Engravers, he was a key link between French Post-Impressionism and the emerging English art movement. He founded the Erangy Press, which produced fine illustrated books printed by hand for 20 years, until war, rising costs and vanishing materials forced its closure.

Pissarro came to know East Anglia after he married Esther Bensusan, in 1892. Early in their marriage the couple lived at Epping, and – even after returning to a base in London – frequently stayed with Esther's relatives in north Essex. At The Minories, Colchester, Pissarro painted in the garden; and he explored the landscapes around Little Easton, near Great Dunmow, and Langham, by the Stour, when visiting the author Samuel Bensusan.

The artist's landscape style and handling of paint, which altered little after 1905, owed much to late work by his father. Essentially an outdoor, *plein air* painter, he built up his scenes by applying solid pigment in separate light-toned coloured touches. His business affairs were shambolic and he was constantly beset by financial difficulties. But through his landscapes there blew a carefree breeze from France.

Lucien Pissarro *River Stour, Stratford St. Mary*, 1934, oil on canvas, 55 × 46cm.

AFTER THE age of 30, New Zealand-born Frances Hodgkins (1869-1947) was travelling almost constantly. Her art appeared in a similar state of flux. She was a successful Post-Impressionist, teaching and painting in Paris at the turn of the century; then, amid moves across England and the Continent, seemed to lose her sense of direction as a painter. Hard times ensued. In later, better years she would regard Cedric Morris and Lett Haines as her rescuers.

Frances Hodgkins *Flatford Mill*, 1930, oil on canvas, 72 × 76cm.

Hodgkins was invited to work with Morris and Haines in London, Cornwall and France; she also received encouragement, introductions to dealers and nomination (from Cedric) for membership of the Seven and Five Society. During the summer of 1930, she paid an extended visit to her friends at their new base in Suffolk and was enchanted by the light, the places and the colours that had once inspired Constable. Many of her pictures consist of still life objects in front of landscapes, but here she abstracted pure compositions of the countryside. Major paintings of Flatford Mill from this period, which shine with energy and atmosphere, are now in the Tate and the Towner Gallery, Eastbourne.

The East Anglian visit also coincided with – and may in part have prompted – the start of the greatest period of this artist's career. Seemingly casual, but in fact very sophisticated, her late pictures pared down scenes from the real world to their essential essences. By the end of her life Frances Hodgkins had secured a prominent place in the tradition of British Romantic art.

willow and gunnera. John Nash had created a plantsman's paradise – a two-acre seed-bed of subjects for the botanical prints and drawings with which he made his name. And from his attic studio, he looked over the garden and a dilapidated barn to the compositions of fields, trees and hedges which were to inspire some ravishing paintings.

A poetic recorder of the natural world, John Northcote Nash was unaffected and largely uninfluenced by theory or example. As a child he had admired John Sell Cotman; and, at first a diffident figure, he had been persuaded to become an artist by his elder brother, Paul. It was the dazzling, metropolitan Paul Nash who also insisted that John's raw facility should not be tamed by tuition. Instead, he pursued his own path as a humorist and landscapist. Moving between the capital and Buckinghamshire, he briefly joined the London Group in 1914, and the Cumberland Market Group (at Harold Gilman's invitation) the following year; then the 1920s found him with the Society of Wood Engravers and the New English Art Club. From Gilman he accepted the advice never to dilute his paint with oil, and to work (at least in the final stages) from drawings rather than direct from nature. But his essential detachment was not breached.

John Nash had been introduced to the landscape of East Anglia on expeditions to Norfolk with the artist Claughton Pellew-Harvey around 1914. In the ensuing turmoil of the First World War, he served first on the Western Front and then as an official war artist with the Ministry of Information. An inner peace was also broken by unrequited passion for Dora Carrington; but the disturbing object of his desires

John Nash, photographed in 1970 working on *Tree in Winter* (opposite page), his paintings, *Fallen Tree*, 1955, watercolour, 25 × 37cm (left) and *Suffolk Harvest*, 1935, oil on canvas, 61 × 89cm (below).

did at least tell him about a fellow student named Christine Kuhlenthal, whom he married in 1918. Revisiting East Anglia soon after the war, he drew and painted at Cromer and Sheringham in Norfolk, and at Wormingford. Needing money, the demobbed artist was obliged to teach at Oxford's Ruskin School of Drawing for much of the 1920s. Between terms he travelled frequently and, from 1929, rented a bungalow beside Wormingford Mill. Two years later, following the destruction of both mill and bungalow in a fire, he took The Thatched Cottage at Wiston by Nayland. East Anglia had hooked him. 'Compared with the West,' he told John Rothenstein, 'it's more brilliant in atmosphere, and it's subtler, less obviously dramatic.' Bottengoms, bought in 1943, became the Nashes' permanent home once John was discharged from war service in the Royal Marines.

Life at Bottengoms settled into a simple and agreeable pattern. Christine – who had painted with Roger Fry's Omega Workshops before her marriage – devoted herself to John's career, ensuring his domestic comfort and scouring the countryside for subjects worth drawing. Their only son, born in 1930, was killed in a car accident at the age of five, and this loss left a shadow over their lives. But Bottengoms became used to the sound of parties and visiting artist

friends included Duncan Grant, Edward Bawden, Gilbert Spencer, Carel Weight, Cedric Morris, Lett Haines and Peter Coker. There were fishing and painting trips to other parts of the country and to the

Continent, and teaching duties at the Royal College, Colchester School of Art and Flatford Mill Field Studies Centre. But John Nash made the secret landscape around Wormingford peculiarly his own.

His technique in oil and watercolour changed little down the decades. He was drawn to intimate East Anglian scenery – the coolness of a wood; the sun ripening small fields of corn; the patterning of furrowed stubble against pyramids of harvested stooks. Although a legendary grumbler, John Nash savoured every part of the annual rural cycle: but in winter, and especially in snow, he was in his element. At Bottengoms the garden and the studio were at one with the rhythm of the seasons. A comforting feeling of return and renewal was also felt during preparation of the six pictures the Royal Academician hung each year in the RA Summer Exhibition.

After the death of Christine, John's health declined sharply, despite the devoted care of Ronald Blythe, whom both had looked upon as a son. He died in hospital in Colchester less than 12 months after his wife of 58 years.

John Nash *The Weir*, **c. 1950, oil on canvas, 76 × 56cm (right) and** *Harvesting*, **1947, 50 × 76cm, reproduced as a poster by School Prints Ltd (below).**

If only for a moment, the north-west corner of Essex – that golden triangle broadly between Great Dunmow, Saffron Walden and Braintree – gives the impression of having stood still, while time rushed on elsewhere. The traffic roaring along the M11 seems a world away from the landscape beyond the motorway verges, where painters have gathered and where the lives of peasant labourers were long captured with lyrical precision by a grand old man of British art.

George Clausen (1852-1944) was born in London, the son of a decorative painter and sculptor of Danish descent. He was apprenticed as a draughts-man in a builder's office, before attending the National Art School in South Kensington. Later,

when working in the studio of Edwin Long, he visited Belgium and Holland, and fell under the spell of the Dutch masters. But is was during studies in Paris that Clausen, like his friend Henry Herbert La Thangue, found his greatest inspiration: the *plein air* painter Bastien-Lepage, whose work was stripped of narrative or moral message to give a literal representation of workers in the field. The rustic naturalism begun in France with Jean François Millet and the Barbizon School had been laid bare. Clausen was intoxicated. On returning to England he left the Royal Academy, where he exhibited in the 1870s, to help found the more radical New English Art Club; and he aban-doned city life, with its encumberance of studio and

George Clausen *The Allotment Garden*, 1899, oil on canvas, 107 × 140cm.

models, to live in the country and work out of doors, recording the lot of the labourer in all conditions. What followed were some of the most striking images of spartan existence in the countryside ever produced in British art: a rendering of Thomas Hardy's novels in paint.

Moving with his wife to Berkshire, Clausen embarked on work in which figures dominated the landscape – their heroic stature often emphasised by a low viewpoint, their forms sharp against a backdrop of soft greens and browns. With a portraitist's eye for character, he might home in on a single worker, or contrast the still-fresh complexion of a boy with the gnarling and weathering on an old man's frost-ruined face. The work of cutting turnips or gathering brush-

George Clausen *The Gleaners,* **1900, watercolour and pastel, 46 × 36cm, and a self portrait, dated 1903.**

wood, of children forced to scare birds or tend sheep in icy solitude, was shown in all its harsh reality, without stinting, without sentimentality.

But by 1891, when he had moved to Widdington, a village five miles south of Saffron Walden, Clausen was aware of the limits of starkest naturalism. During the late 1880s, his work had echoed the square brush work of Bastien-Lepage, and his larger pictures had been uniformly suffused with a grey even light. Then he discovered Degas' pastels and began to explore the immediacy of this sketching medium for himself: this encouraged a clearer expression of local colour, a greater sense of movement and, most of all, an appreciation of iridescent light. More and more he became fascinated by the monumental and the general, rather than the particular; and, from painting figures in a scene, he drew back and widened his field of vision, to depict landscapes with figures and, finally, empty panoramas. The wide expanses of East Anglia were perfect for his purpose.

The artist also revised his decision to work direct from nature: the fleeting appearance of things, the rarity of repeated light and a prevalence of grey and overcast days persuaded him to resort to the techniques of memory, sketchbooks and photographs (his earliest studies predate those of the great cameraman of Broadland, P. H. Emerson). He followed the plough, jotting down notes of the human body in motion, before returning to the studio to paint. But even then he was never a complete countryman:

except for a brief interlude, he spent part of each year in London, where he retained a studio in St John's Wood, lectured (he was professor of painting at the Royal Academy Schools 1904-6 and later its director) and wrote books on art theory. He was fêted by his peers and knighted for his services to painting in 1927.

Clausen left Widdington in 1905, but renewed his ties with north-west Essex 12 years later, purchasing a house named Hillside, at Duton Hill. At the bottom of his orchard he converted a small shed into a studio and here he worked on a wealth of subjects drawn from the surrounding farms, lanes and villages.

He liked the 'opaque' method of painting, where the dried pigment is applied thick and not as a transparent glaze over a luminous ground. To avoid heaviness he had to achieve an exceptional vitality of colour, and did so using primary tones laid on unmixed with small strokes of the brush. This brilliant device captured the Impressionist ideal of seizing the immediate aspect of a subject and the vibrant effects of light. The artist also gained an increasing freedom in watercolour, explaining his favourite technique in 1930: 'I try (though, of course, I can seldom do it) to put the colour on in one wash, without retouching, for I think there is nothing so

George Clausen *Our Blacksmith*, **1931, oil on canvas, 75 × 90cm. Shown at work in the forge at Great Easton are Mr Turner, the village blacksmith (left), his assistant Mr Rolph (right) and, in the background, Mr Hayden. For posing in his Great War Puttees Mr Rolph was paid 2s6d.**

beautiful as a clean tint in watercolour that is exactly right. And even if it does not exactly run into the right place (for watercolour is a tricky medium) the quality of the colour has something of the spontaneity and effortless rightness that one finds in Nature itself – a quality that is always lost by labouring and stippling a drawing.'

His transition from what might be called cold to poetic realism was mirrored in a move from painting the unmysterious light of day to the misty beauty of sunrise and sunset. One of several similar scenes painted in the 1920s, *Sunrise in September*, uses a road crossing the foreground of the picture and going behind the ricks to lead the eye to the focal point in the group of trees and the horizon. Such conventional arrangements show Clausen's fine sense of design. The surface of the picture (painted dryly and thickly on an absorbent ground) echoes the powdery texture of frost. In 1931 he revealed his routine for painting a sunrise: 'I go out half an hour before sunrise and paint

George Clausen *Sunset*, **1920, oil on canvas, 35 × 46cm (above) and** *Sunrise*, **c. 1924, oil on canvas, 61 × 76cm (right).**

till half an hour after sunrise. If the weather is favourable, I do it every morning, say, for a fortnight. By that time I get all I am likely to get out of it. Then I go indoors and paint. Perhaps I produce a picture – and perhaps I don't.' In contrast, from 1897, a fascination with the problems of painting with a strong *chiaroscuro* – a stress on light and shade – led him to execute a series of pictures of boys winnowing and threshing in dark barns, followed much later by studies of the blacksmith's forge at Great Easton.

Until his death at the age of 92, George Clausen always endeavoured to push his art further. His style showed an increasing fluidity as the years advanced; and though his key subject was the life and landscape around his country homes, at various times he also evoked nudes, allegorical works, portraits and interiors. Clausen's myriad pictures captured the moment and also served as lasting points of reference for many painters who were to follow.

North-west Essex also lured two young artists who, on a cycling trip in 1928, came upon the village of Great Bardfield and its fine main street of historic houses. At once enchanted, they were allowed to rent half of a Georgian building named Brick House, for use initially as a weekend and holiday retreat from London. Edward Bawden and Eric Ravilious were the first and most prominent among a group of artists who settled in the village during and after the war years. But these painters and craftsmen would be linked by friendship, creative versatility and in most cases a strong response to the landscape, rather than by similarities of style.

Edward Bawden (1903-89) always belonged here. He was born in Braintree, the only son of a Methodist ironmonger, and attended Saffron Walden's Quaker school. Apart from work and studies in London, holidays and roving adventures as a war artist in France, Africa and the Middle East, he stayed unusually close to his birthplace. The boundaries of his childhood – the contours of the countryside, vernacular architecture and deep local traditions of puritanism – shaped the vast variety of

Edward Bawden *Cattlemarket, Braintree,* **1937,** linocut, **54 × 82cm.**

his art. Their abiding importance also pointed to a remarkable self-sufficiency: it has rightly been noted that few if any other artists have stamped their imprint so firmly on the modern scene, while remaining so untouched by contemporaries, movements and fashions. Bawden's style was his own, yet, inevitably, there were early influences. There was, for example, the complex humour exhibited in so much of his work: by turns caustic, malicious and mischievous, it may have hinted at an underlying melancholy. At the Cambridge School of Art, the wit and invention of the gifted student's sometimes fantastical drawings paid homage to Beardsley; during refinement at London's Royal College of Art, an absurdity of subject recalled Edward Lear. But overall and over time, onion-like layers of quirky comedy

evolved which were pure Bawden. In marvellous watercolours, too, the artist's unique vision was in part focused by others – besides the parallel journey with Ravilious, key markers were provided by Paul Nash (a visiting tutor at the RCA) and his brother, John.

After enrolling at the RCA to study calligraphy and illumination, Edward Bawden found swift acclaim as a graphic designer. A pictorial map for the Empire Exhibition at Wembley was followed by London Underground posters, and then by a flood of amusing advertisements, calendars, book jackets, illustrations and greeting cards. Between 1928 and 1930 he worked with Ravilious, his friend and fellow design student, on wax-tempera murals for London's Morley College; this project proving the first of

Edward Bawden *Screen*, **commissioned in 1950 for the Festival of Britain exhibition on London's South Bank.**

several successful sorties into the area of large-scale decorative art. But despite the exuberance of much of his work, the retiring Bawden needed the security of his native landscape. On marrying the potter Charlotte Epton, in 1932, he received Brick House as a wedding present from his father. The couple, at first together with Ravilious and his wife, the wood engraver and painter Tirzah Garwood, made the building their permanent home.

In Essex, Bawden followed Ravilious in perfecting the art of watercolour. Some of the pair's first local landscapes were executed when the roof of their home was being repaired; they climbed on to the ridge and painted the views around them. Then home, garden, village street, nearby fields and farms were scoured for subjects. For an artist who remained essentially a linear draughtsman, Bawden developed a distinctive painting technique. According to his friend and sometime Bardfield neighbour, the painter, teacher and print-maker Michael Rothenstein, he possessed 'the remarkable ability of reducing complex forms to a direct shorthand pattern of brush-strokes; from the large shapes down to small details this sprightly calligraphy is sustained.' Bawden chose to draw on non-absorbent paper with a very hard and sharp pencil; washes would then be superimposed one upon another, to build up luminous layers – like oil-paint glazes – of deep colour. Often the texture and underlying pigment was enhanced by scratching through and drawing on the surface. Skies dominate his work as they do the East Anglian landscape and were usually the last part of the picture to be completed. Sometimes Bawden's clouds seem like broken chunks of solid matter, their once-interlocking shapes forced apart by rivulets of white paper. The drama overhead emphasises the placid nature of the scenery below. Overall, the early watercolours were often lyrical; but gradually the artist developed a tougher mode of working, so that the painting appeared altogether tighter, with constant underpinning by that teasingly satirical or sardonic wit.

Eric Ravilious (1903-42) was born in London but moved when a child to Eastbourne, whose school of art was to be his first training ground. His inspiration came in large part from the landscape of the Sussex Downs: wind-blown, chalk-white, lonely and luminous, its image haunts his work. An echo was found in remote East Anglia. Ravilious mastered a range of media, being a major figure in the revival of wood engraving in the 1920s, a lithographer for book illustrations, and an industrial and commercial designer for posters and advertisements, furniture, ceramics, textiles and glass. In every field he exploited

Edward Bawden *Brick House Garden Party*, 1932, pen and ink drawing, 20 × 28cm. The artist is seated next to Tirzah Garwood, opposite Eric Ravilious and diagonally opposite Thomas Hennell.

a brilliant sense of design: his watercolour landscapes, domestic studies and greenhouse interiors were experiments with colours and shapes, their formal power heightened by an atmosphere of eerie emptiness. In this artist's work a human presence is generally limited to the distant past: in East Anglia he delighted in decrepit machinery, rusting in yards and ditches.

In 1934 Ravilious and his wife moved from Brick House to Bank House, Castle Hedingham, a ten-mile bicycle ride from Great Bardfield. He shunned the sort of scenery that he felt had been recorded by others, but sought out fresh fields where surprises could still be sprung. And, anxious that his palette was too muted and gloomy, he strove for more dynamic harmonies of colour. For example, he was displeased by a watercolour of a baker's cart seen through the window of his front-room studio. 'This picture IS a bit too pale,' he wrote, 'and whenever I see the cart opposite in full daffodil yellow, I wish I'd laid on the colour more.' Of a later landscape, he added: 'I so want the thing not to look washed out as they so often do.' Like Bawden, Ravilious was a savage critic of his own work. His finished pictures exude a sense of calm facility, but great efforts were taken in execution, and subjects could be repeated many times until they were judged adequate. After his death, his wife wrote that he 'showed on an average only one out of every four or five paintings he produced, tearing up the failures. It wasn't until his third show at Tooth's in 1939 that he felt satisfied that he had really achieved something.' The critics were united in praise. Jan Gordon's review for *The Sunday Times* of that London exhibition still stands as the best thumbnail sketch of the painter's appeal: 'Between the acts of seeing and perceiving a gulf lies. Of talented artists the majority do but see, clearly perhaps, hypnotically sometimes, but moments of extra-perception are rare. Of these watercolours by Ravilious one may feel that a large number of them do touch true perception. No matter what the subject may be, a sandpit, a country lane in a drizzle, a broken water-turbine lying in a stream, the window of a pub-room with a spangled ceiling, a farmhouse bedroom, an old boat on the mud . . . each by a combination of unexpected selection, exactly apt colour, and an almost prestidigitous watercolour technique and textural variety, appear as something magic, almost mystic, distilled out of the ordinary everyday.'

The search for things out of the ordinary and

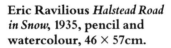

Eric Ravilious *Halstead Road in Snow,* **1935, pencil and watercolour, 46 × 57cm.**

everyday drew Ravilious to dramatic effects of weather; he recorded floods and blizzards and, like Bawden, enjoyed painting directly into the sun. In 1940 he was appointed an official war artist, first with the Admiralty and later with the Royal Air Force. Amid sketching tours from base to base, and following a short posting to Norway, Ravilious managed to move his family to Ironbridge Farm, in the Pant Valley, at Shalford, near Braintree. He had scant time to appreciate the lush local countryside. His duties continued to take him all over the country until, at the end of August 1942, he was successful in a bid to join the Norwegian Squadron in Iceland.

The glacial terrain and uncannily long sunsets would have delighted him, but we can only guess at the work that might have resulted. Within a week of

T HE ICELAND posting left vacant by the death of Ravilious was secured by one of the late artist's closest friends during his Essex years. **Thomas Hennell** (1903-45) had charged by chance into the lives of the Brick House painters when, en route to Norfolk, he was given a bed for the night by their landlady. Edward Bawden recalled: 'One morning in 1931 when Eric Ravilious and I came down to the kitchen in Brick House to wash ourselves we found a stranger, stripped to the waist, pumping water over his head and making quite a splash in the large slate sink. He was tall, thin with black beady eyes rather close set, dark slightly curly hair, and as he greeted us his voice had a deep booming parsonic ring, echoed even more loudly when he laughed. Outside, leaning against the doorpost was a heavy, khaki coloured Army bike and on it, tied to the bar between the saddle and steering wheel, a large and perfect specimen of a corn dollie, of the sort called the Lord's table. Tom greeted us in the most friendly manner. Our identity was divulged in a matter of seconds and friendship established immediately.' Frequent visits followed; the pattern resuming after Hennell's sudden mental breakdown and treatment for schizophrenia in Claybury Hospital, Essex.

A Kent rector's son, Thomas Barclay Hennell was a tortured figure, who poured a love of the countryside into poems, prose and pictures of passionate intensity. His mission to record the age-old tools and traditions of agricultural and rural life was a race against time. He had found Brick House while collecting material for his first book, *Change in the Farm,* an almanac which described a 1930s farmhouse and the ancient arts of land management and animal husbandry still practised by the occupants. Later visits brought friendship with the ruralist writer C. Henry Warren, who lived at Finchingfield; Hennell's illustrations for the latter's war-time volumes on barely mechanised farmwork, *The Land is Yours* and *Miles from Anywhere* — were drawn from north-west Essex subjects. Intervening volumes, covering country crafts, left an epitaph for a society of rural artisans being rendered obsolete by modern mass production.

Hennell aimed at objective documentation but possessed a deep affinity with the things he portrayed. As the artist's biographer, Michael Macleod, puts it: 'His drawings of rural subjects are founded on crafts – his own skills and the skills depicted. Hennell understood and respected all that he drew, and his painstaking thoroughness produced an art of disciplined integrity.' For some of his most effective drawings of figures and implements, he broke off the point of a pencil and dipped the stump in ink. But it was as a landscape watercolourist that he won most note, being elected a member of the Royal Watercolour Society in 1943. He was a superb war artist, and his paintings of Iceland, Normandy and the Far East suggest the wealth of work that should have followed. But, just days after the Japanese surrender, Thomas Hennell disappeared in Indonesia and was never seen again.

Thomas Hennell *The Land is Yours,* 1945, a watercolour design for a book jacket.

his arrival, Eric Ravilious was lost on board an Air Sea Rescue plane which failed to return from a mission. The widowed Tirzah moved with her three children first to Wethersfield and then, on remarrying, to London. She died at Copford, near Colchester, in 1951.

Although torpedoed off the coast of West Africa, Edward Bawden survived the war unscathed. Returning to rural Essex, he continued to deploy the skills of an artisan and master craftsman, inventing and adapting special devices to overcome technical problems arising from the attempt to relate his precise vision. Over the years he made clever use of mixed media, drawing with crayon over paint, for instance, or applying heel-ball to paper, damping it and then ironing it over a sheet of blotting-paper to soak up surplus wax and achieve a matt surface. Like Ravilious, he frequently employed a penknife or razor-blade, to scratch out lights or snow flakes; and he embellished a mural for Queen's University, Belfast, with 20,000 nails. But it was in the medium of the lino-cut that the artist may have been most innovative – slicing and gouging out intricate detail and delicate contrasts of texture; his famous posters for schools, most of his exquisite book jackets and many other illustrations were created with this supposedly crude medium. Again, the spirit of unspoilt Essex pervaded the work. In books such as *Good Food* and *Life in an English Village,* Bawden displayed an intimate knowledge of church services, flower and vegetable shows, fetes and harvest festivals – the very fabric of community life in the countryside. The gaiety of his art meant that, with Ravilious in the 1930s, he added an East Anglian flavour to national celebrations, such as royal coronations. For the 1951 Festival of Britain, he produced a screen of 12 high, narrow panels, recording rural pursuits, mansions, cottages, churches, pubs and railway stations, nestled amid woods and fields strewn with labourers, rooks, cows, and the much-loved Bawden emblem of a cat; light contrasted with dark; diagonal furrows being ploughed in one panel become a steeply pitched roof in the next. Sadly dismantled after the exhibition, the screen resembled a folk art design for a stained glass

John Aldridge *The Pink Farm,* **1940, oil on board, 33 × 46cm.**

window. Bawden was assisted in the project by artist neighbours Walter Hoyle (later to build up the print department at the Cambridge College of Art), Sheila Robinson (tutor in illustration at the Royal College of Art, noted printer on cardboard and mother of the artist Chloe Cheese) and John Aldridge – the latter was to prove a particularly important collaborator.

London-born **John Aldridge** (1905-83) moved with his wife, Lucie, to The Place House at Great Bardfield in 1933 and remained there for the rest of his life. He was already a successful oil painter on arrival in Essex, having exhibited richly-coloured landscapes and still lifes with the Seven and Five Society and at his first one-man show with London's Leicester Galleries. Bawden then persuaded him to experiment with lino-cuts. In 1938 the two men jointly launched Bardfield Wallpapers, producing a series of bold designs loosely based around rural motifs, cutting the sets of linoleum blocks needed for printing in several colours and printing off the first pieces. This exhausting venture, intended for commercial manufacture, was killed off by the outbreak of war.

Without any formal art training, Aldridge had taken up painting when a student at Oxford. His very personal pictures were uninfluenced by fashionable or commercial concerns, but were produced purely for his own pleasure and for that of his friends. Creative curiosity and technical dexterity enabled him to excel in fields as diverse as book illustration

John Aldridge *Autumn*, **1946, oil on canvas, 51 × 61cm.**

Michael Rothenstein *Landscape with Church and Chickens*, **1942, watercolour and pen.**

and textile design. He also proved a sympathetic teacher, becoming an assistant at the Slade under William Coldstream in 1949. His pictures won international notice after being shown at the 1934 Venice Biennale, and he exhibited regularly at the Royal Academy. In 1963 he was elected an Academician.

At heart, John Aldridge – even more than the keen gardener Edward Bawden – was an expert and dedicated plantsman. His main project over half a century lay in creating at The Place a glorious garden beside a stream, with giant hogweeds and huge herbaceous borders which owed much to the pioneering spirit of Gertrude Jekyll. Providing an apt setting for an idyllic Elizabethan plaster and timber house, this labour of love was to prove Aldridge's finest work of art and his sympathetic tribute to the fertility of the

north-west Essex landscape. Inevitably, it also inspired paintings of deep emotion and a poetry almost akin to the writing of his great friend Robert Graves.

The Place was blessed with its own chapel, and it was here that **Michael Rothenstein** (b. 1908) and his portraitist wife Duffy (who later married artist Eric Ayers) went to live in 1941. Shortly afterwards the couple settled at Ethel House, a stone's throw from Brick House. The younger son of Sir William Rothenstein (and brother of John) had enjoyed a privileged artistic background, from which he had emerged as a student of promise, rivalling his friend Edward Burra. But at 18 he was struck down by a debilitating illness, so that his energies and spirit were sapped for several years. Eventual recovery was akin to a rebirth. Michael Rothenstein looked at the world afresh, with an eye for spotting the significance of previously overlooked detail (sign-posts, ploughs and cockerels became recurring motifs) and a feverish creativity. For a while he was influenced by the Neo-Romantic movement and sketched with Stanley Spencer, but his images were too disparate and too personal to be tied to a single school. He has imbued his pictures with a tension at times bordering on threat, by featuring opposing forms: the natural and the mechanical, the domestic and the untamed. Some of his finest work warns of the landscape's ruination. In all, Rothenstein's diverse output has been united by an openness to his surroundings and an exhilaration at what the artist has called the 'sudden intrusions of the marvellous into the everyday'.

When he moved to Essex, Michael Rothenstein was working for the Recording Britain scheme organised by the Pilgrim Trust, as was another wartime resident of Bardfield, Kenneth Rowntree. Later, both men also produced colour lithographs of Essex subjects for the School Prints series, with Rothenstein offering a study of timber felling and Rowntree depicting a tractor. From being a painter in oil, gouache, watercolour and collage, of landscape and figure subjects, Michael Rothenstein became increasingly interested in print-making. He wanted an immediacy of expression and, naturally, was urged by Bawden to try out pieces of linoleum and a penknife. But in the 1950s the artist untapped a startling inven-

tiveness of technique, and scintillating use of colour, helped not a little by visits to the Paris studio of S. W. Hayter. Founding his own graphic workshop at Ethel House, before a later move to Stisted, near Braintree, Rothenstein revolutionised the process of print-making. His blocks were culled from a rag and bone yard collection of found objects (often salvaged from local rubbish tips): wood, metal, plaster and even fabric – anything that could be coated with ink. Among his early students was George Chapman, who lived at Great Bardfield between 1948 and 1960, but who is now best known for stark paintings, etchings and drawings of south Wales.

Brick House remained the focal point of Bardfield creativity. Edward and Charlotte Bawden, with their artist offspring Richard and Joanna, made their home a meeting place, a makeshift college and a gallery. In the 1950s, thanks to their example, several houses in the village were thrown open for highly successful exhibitions of local work. But within a few years the community began to disperse as the remoteness of north-west Essex diminished. In 1970, after the death of his wife, Edward Bawden moved to a little house in Saffron Walden, which he crammed with the remnants of a long and still-continuing career. In old age his landscapes became more and more localised, until confined almost entirely to domestic scenes. But he remained throughout an Essex puritan poking affectionate fun at his surroundings.

Michael Rothenstein *Essex Plough*, 1947, watercolour and ink, 39 × 56cm.

In addition to the pull of Great Bardfield, Essex has attracted a number of artists whose work, especially during the 1940s, was termed Neo-Romantic. They looked back to the subjects and techniques of early nineteenth-century painters – notably Blake, Constable, Cotman, Palmer and Turner – and used landscape to project emotions. A pervading sense of melancholy in their pictures was well suited to a time of war and its shell-shocked aftermath.

None of the Neo-Romantics was more versatile, erudite and dogmatic than the razor sharp **Michael Ayrton** (1921-75) – he took the name of his Labour MP mother because the 'A' would give him prominence at mixed exhibitions. Ayrton spread – some say frittered – a prodigious talent through work as a public personality and controversialist. He was a critic, broadcaster, novelist, art historian, theatrical designer and film director, as well as a painter, sculptor and etcher. His art spanned Biblical, mythological and erotic themes; he borrowed from Graham Sutherland, Paul Nash – in studies of tangled roots and tree trunks taking human form – and Picasso, whom he nevertheless blasted as 'The Master of Pastiche'. And he answered attacks on his own astringent,

sculptural pictures. 'A critic has accused me of applying paint like a skilful housepainter', he once wrote, 'and I take no exception to this since I am concerned with rendering images as simply and austerely as I am able and not in producing delectable or succulent pictorial dishes.'

London-born Ayrton had a formal education broken by serious illness, but briefly attended several art schools. At 17 he settled in Paris with John Minton (another Neo-Romantic painter, born in 1917 at Great Shelford, near Cambridge). With the outbreak of war, he joined the RAF but was invalided out in 1942. He secured a post teaching life drawing and theatre design at Camberwell and his career began to take off in all directions.

In 1951 Ayrton, with his wife and three stepdaughters, left London for Essex. He had purchased Bradfields, near Toppesfield – a fine house which he had visited as a child. Part of its attraction was the ready-made sculptor's studio provided by a large, concrete-floored barn where advice from Henry Moore and Alberto Giacometti was put to good use in arguably the artist's most important work. Here he tackled several rural themes. A briefly renewed

Michael Ayrton *Essex Hedges,* 1953, oil, 71 × 89cm.

interest in landscape painting led to icily atmospheric pictures of the 1950s such as *Winter, Figures in Snow* and *Snowbird*. Breaking his earlier rule, he completed still lifes of fruit, hams and vegetables which were both delectable and succulent. And, in drawings, oils and prints, he returned to studies of lamb-carrying shepherds he had begun in Italy. Although bathed in an unearthly light, these figures bear the look of authentic East Anglian farm labourers.

While continuing to travel widely and to display daunting energy, Michael Ayrton enjoyed retreating into the Essex countryside until the end of his life. Here he could work without interruption. His plans remained at full pace when he suffered a fatal heart attack, after driving to his London flat. He is buried in Hadstock Church, near Saffron Walden.

Other visitors to north-east Essex have included two Scottish painters now merged into the public memory as one. 'The two Roberts' – Colquhoun and MacBryde – became inseparable after first meeting at the Glasgow School of Art. In London from 1941, both freed from military service on medical grounds, they shared a studio with John Minton and later were briefly the darlings of the London art scene. They drew on Wyndham Lewis, Jankel Adler, Braque and Picasso, to produce pictures of tragic outlook, taut design and strange, sombre colour divisions (brighter in MacBryde's case). Their semi-Cubist broken images, reassembled in interlocking shards, seemed a timely metaphor for the devastation of war. From early landscapes, **Robert Colquhoun** (1914-62) reached a peak with moving studies of the human figure, while **Robert MacBryde** (1913-66) perfected sharply outlined still lifes. But Colquhoun was always the acknowledged master, and MacBryde (born Mac-Bride) the housekeeper and promoter of his partner's career. They would also fight famously, drink excessively and fall apart together.

As an escape from war-time London, they made frequent trips to the country. Their hosts in Essex were the painters Richard Chopping and Dennis Wirth-Miller at Wivenhoe. Landscapes and river drawings completed here include Colquhoun's Sutherland-influenced *Essex Orchard*. Less than a decade later, when ejected from their London flat and about to be rejected by their dealer, the Roberts made for Tilty. This tiny hamlet near Great Dunmow was rife with artists. The writer Louis MacNeice had a house here, while Elizabeth Smart (author of the brilliant prose poem *By Grand Central Station I Sat Down And Wept*) and her four children by the poet George Barker, occupied Tilty Mill. The mill was at one time sub-let by the surrealist poet Ruthven Todd, who had invited the Neo-Romantic painter John Craxton and Lucian Freud to stay there. Elizabeth, working on a magazine in London during the week,

let Colquhoun and MacBryde share Tilty Mill – on condition that they helped to look after the children. For almost three years, from the summer of 1951, the Roberts lived there, often visited by Soho friends, such as poets Dylan Thomas, Paul Potts and W. S. Graham and the photographer John Deakin. Inevitably, there were also wild drinking bouts and violent arguments, which left both Roberts bruised, windows smashed and furniture damaged. In the end Elizabeth Smart had to tell her lodgers to go, and was left to settle their colossal pub bill. But the Barker children would remember their gentleness, patience and skill at inventing wonderful games. Sebastian Barker has remarked that too much has been made of the pair's drinking: taken up when young by the art world and then dropped, they were forced to develop consolatory devices.

At Tilty, the Roberts worked swiftly in a garden studio, which the children later recalled as a marvellously evocative place, with its rows of canvases and smell of oil paint. Colquhoun, in particular, portrayed the cats, dogs, goats and horses around him. He also became engrossed in painting pigs at a neighbouring farm. One animal was ruthlessly dissected in an offset drawing and oil study, and also features in the sizeable *Figures in a Farmyard* painting of 1953.

The Roberts next descended on East Anglia to visit an old friend, Bobby Hunt, at Groton, near Sudbury, towards the end of 1957. By now they were both alcoholic and destitute. For most of the following year, as Colquhoun first prepared for his retrospective at the Whitechapel Gallery, and then drank the profits, Hunt provided a roof and an etching press; but his patience ran out when Colquhoun

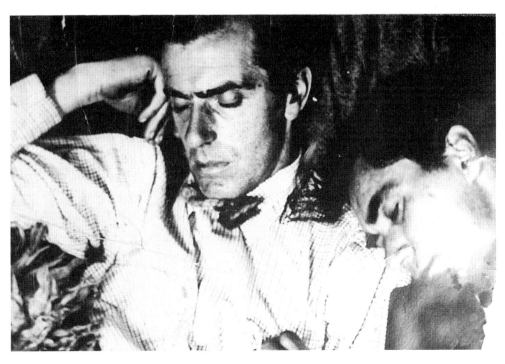

The two Roberts: Colquhoun (left) and MacBryde (right) at Tilty.

Robert Colquhoun *Pig*, c. 1952,
oil on canvas, 30 × 40cm.

threw a lighted paraffin lamp. The local vicar secured temporary accommodation until, early in 1959, a removal to The Ancient House, Kersey, was recorded in a short documentary film by Ken Russell. But even this idyllic refuge could not last. In *Dead As Doornails,* Anthony Cronin tells how MacBryde returned to London claiming to have burnt the house with his lover in it. Colquhoun, of course, turned up a few days later. After that they continued to drift around old haunts until Colquhoun's death from a heart attack in 1962. Four years later, MacBryde, reduced to a husk, was knocked down by a car and killed after a drinking session in Dublin.

Another painter attracted to the Neo-Romantic movement and to the feel of East Anglia, was **Keith Vaughan** (1912-77). David Thompson wrote of Vaughan in a 1962 Whitechapel catalogue: 'In Minton and Colquhoun he found artists concerned as

he was with human subjects and particularly with that strange mixture of social documentary, of recording the day-to-day routine of people living in a besieged island, and a sort of tortured, prickly romanticism, which characterised so much English art of the forties.' Born in Sussex, and moving as an infant to London, he attended no formal art school, but at 19 joined the Unilever advertising agency, Lintas, to train as a layout artist. A friendship developed with John Passmore and both trainees stayed at Gooseberry Cottage, Lindsey Tye, near Hadleigh – the Suffolk retreat of their art director, Reg Jenkins, and his wife, the painter Marjorie Jenkins. The Australian Passmore, like his compatriot Arthur Boyd, came to admire East Anglian landscape; during prolonged periods at Lindsey Tye he paid homage to Cézanne in paintings of the house, orchard and surrounding cornfields. Vaughan also made return trips to Suffolk in 1948 and into the 1950s. Only then, despite life-long self-doubt, did he consider himself to be a true painter.

In 1939 Vaughan had taken a year off to develop his art in rural Surrey. Always isolated and uncertain, he was plunged into personal crisis by the war, eventually registering as a conscientious objector and building roads across Salisbury Plain and the Wye Valley with the Pioneer Corps. His pictures, mainly gouache and ink and pencil drawings at this time, were purchased by the War Artists Advisory Committee. Demobbed in 1946, he shared a house with John Minton, who encouraged his painting and found him a teaching post at Camberwell. At last he began to work seriously with oils. Over time his main subject of bullet-headed boys in lonely scenery was simplified into depersonalised figures failing to make contact amid a stark landscape of sloping rectangles. But until the end, he abstracted his firmly structured pictures from life.

Keith Vaughan often visited the Ayrtons at Bradfields, and in 1964 he bought a row of farm labourers' cottages nearby. The vacant terrace had been condemned; floors had to be lowered and ceilings stripped back to their seventeenth-century beams, before the dwellings could be rebuilt into a single house. His partner then looked after the place and Vaughan stayed for weekends and holidays. A few painter friends came too, including David Hockney and Patrick Procktor. During walks to the village shop or pub, or when driving into Sudbury, Vaughan would stop and make rough landscape sketches which would be worked up into paintings in his Toppesfield or London studios. The off-white blocks of local farmhouses, set amid bare ploughed ochre fields, inspired some unpeopled canvases. The habitually subdued greens were brightened here by cobalt-green – the colour of agricultural machinery (though the added expense and persisting aim for austerity meant that such dabs were used sparingly).

Vaughan's journals confirm the unhappy and tormented soul hinted at in his painting. He held on to a wry humour, but was increasingly depressed, deflected and despairing; finally, when seriously ill, in 1977, he took his life.

Keith Vaughan *Troy's Farm*, 1960, oil on board, 41 × 43cm (right) – the farm is situated near the village of Great Yeldham, and *Bulmer Tye*, 1972, oil on board, 45 × 40cm (below). Bulmer Tye is a hamlet situated south west of Sudbury.

Boating on the Cam was a blissful way to float through the sweltering summer afternoons of 1910. Hiring a craft at Cambridge and rowing away from the town – hurriedly past Sheeps' Green and Coe Fen, while ladies among the party shielded their eyes from the sight of boys bathing naked – a moderate oarsman could reach the village of Grantchester with ease. A meandering journey, beyond meadows blotched by fat cattle and fringed with elms and pollard willows, might end at a mooring place near the millpool. From the river bank, a footpath led to The Orchard, then – and until 1987 – tea-rooms, with tables set out beneath apple trees. Often present was a group of students presided over by a young man lodging at The Old Vicarage next door, who was already famous for his Adonis looks and whose

poems would soon be immortalised by his death in the First World War. Rupert Brooke's coterie might include his lover, Ka Cox, plus a young French artist named Jacques Raverat and his fiancée, Gwendolen Mary Darwin. Rationalist thinkers and free spirits, they were shaking off Victorian restraint.

Gwen Raverat (1885–1957), though painfully shy in company, went on to produce wonderfully uninhibited images of the people and places in and around her native town. She was born into a large and gifted family. Her father, Sir George Darwin, was professor of astronomy at Cambridge University; her grandfather was the evolutionist Charles Darwin. One forebear was the potter Josiah Wedgwood and the composer Ralph Vaughan Williams (for whose Masque for Dancing ballet she later designed sets and

Rupert Brooke and friends in The Orchard, Grantchester, c. 1910 with Gwen Darwin left (?).

costumes) was a cousin. The family provided an enclosed and eccentric world. And if, inevitably, there were nursery restrictions, there were also fine houses to explore amid a setting where the country still infiltrated the town. From her home by the river, the young Gwen Darwin would watch cattle being driven across the ford at Newnham, to and from the milking stables, and corn sacks being hoisted into King's Mill (demolished in 1928), near Silver Street Bridge. At that time Cambridge was enveloped in the smell of horses – or worse. In *Period Piece,* her brilliant memoir of childhood, the artist recalled that until the mid-1890s raw sewage had gone straight into the Cam. Unlike her American mother – who had written after arriving in Cambridge: 'I am at last in the Utopia of all my fondest dreams' – Gwen's witty and affectionate vision was rooted in robust reality.

Drawing from life by the age of ten, the artist produced work at once naturalistic and atmospheric. Although she attended painting classes at the Slade, from 1908, she was soon teaching herself wood engraving – after basic instruction from her cousin by marriage, Elinor Monsell Darwin, and inspiration from the Georgian master Thomas Bewick. Her technique, for both hard and soft woods, was to use a range of engraver tools on the end of the grain, rather than applying a knife to the plank. Her hallmark was the creation of form by the fall of light and shadow – such an echo of Impressionism being enhanced by two spells in France. After marrying Jacques Raverat, she lived first at Croydon-cum-Clapton, in the Cambridgeshire countryside near Royston. Then, as her husband's health failed, there was a brief move to Le Havre, in 1915, with a later period in the south of France from 1920 to 1925. While nursing Jacques

Gwen Raverat *The Fen,* **1935, wood engraving, 18 × 15cm.**

IN THE SUMMER of 1909, a meadow at Grantchester was strewn with a raggle-taggle encampment of caravans, horses, tents and wild children, amid which moved the unmistakable figures of **Augustus John** (1878-1961) and his lover Dorelia McNeill. Imitating their gypsy heroes, the family of nomads had processed from Epsom, pulled towards Cambridge by a commission to paint the Greek scholar Jane Harrison (a project promoted by Ruth Darwin, cousin of Gwen). En route, John had noted that 'respectable people become indignant at the sight of us – and disrespectable ones behave charmingly'. Prim Cambridge was to be cut to the quick, still more so when the bearded Bohemian brawled in the street with his groom. In turn, John – as bold, vital and colourful as his paintings – sniffed at university life. 'The atmosphere of those venerable halls standing in such peaceful and dignified seclusion,' the painter wrote in his autobiography, *Chiaroscuro,* 'seemed to me likely to induce a state of languor and reverie, excluding both the rude shocks and the joyous revelations of the rough world without.'

The portrait completed, the tribe moved to Norwich. Here, on a piece of waste ground by the river, it was abandoned by its chief, who left by train to paint the Lord Mayor of Liverpool. When John returned, his followers proved exhausted by camp-life; the horses were ailing and the insolent groom was finally dismissed. They limped on as far as Sea Palling, then sought refuge on the farm of a friend, Charles Slade, at Thurning – where the children promptly went down with whooping cough. At that point the lure of Chelsea was too tempting to resist.

through the final stages of his illness, she never stopped drawing and engraving.

Returning to England a widow with two young daughters, Gwen Raverat lived for three years in London, before settling near Cambridge, at The Old Rectory, Harlton. The surrounding scenes prompted some fine illustrations – for A. G. Street's *Farmer's Glory* and *Mountains And Molehills,* by her cousin Frances Cornford – while the spirit of local places infused projects such as the 1932 *Cambridge Book of Poetry for Children,* edited by Kenneth Grahame. She also loved pure fantasy, executing coloured engravings for *Bird Talisman,* a Victorian story by her great-uncle Harry Wedgwood. Her lively pen and ink work reached a peak in 1952 with her drawings for the best-selling *Period Piece,* by which time she was back in Cambridge itself, living in The Old Granary, in the garden of her childhood home.

In 1920 Gwen Raverat had helped found the Society of Wood Engravers, with John Nash, Lucien Pissarro and Eric Gill. But her own work remained idiosyncratic – distinct, especially, from the stylised and much-copied designs of her friend Gill. She was a fairly prolific book illustrator in the 1930s, and continued her engraving career until she suffered a stroke while completing the *Period Piece* drawings.

Otherwise, this descendant of acute hypochondriacs shrugged off disability. In her last days she produced small oil paintings, still glowing with life and light.

During the 1930s Gwen Raverat devised sets and costumes for productions of Handel operas at the Cambridge Guildhall. For a time her collaborator was **Elisabeth Vellacott** (b. 1905) – formerly an assistant scene painter at the Old Vic, under Lilian Baylis, and a designer for the Cambridge University Musical Society's 1931 production of Purcell's *The Fairy Queen* (in which James Mason, then an undergraduate, played Oberon). But most – and more important – work by these very different artists derived from the landscape.

Elisabeth Vellacott was born at Grays, Essex, a stone's throw from the Thames and, although her childhood was divided between London, Cambridge and a boarding school in Lincolnshire, a river has rarely been far from her life and work. In 1959 she settled beside the Ouse, in a light-filled, triangular-shaped house built in an old orchard, at Hemingford Grey – close to her friend, the writer Lucy Boston. But other influences on her art were widely drawn. Before the age of ten she was sketching watercolour trees and sunsets from a window of the family home in Cambridge (where her father was studying to be

Elisabeth Vellacott *The People Passing By,* 1988, oil on panel, 61 × 79cm.

ordained). Landscape painting followed during Cotswold holidays. At the Royal College of Art, between 1925 and 1929, a fellow student was the painter Cecil Collins, who later also moved to Cambridge. Both held fast to figurative work. But whereas Collins called up mystical, dream-like creations from an interior world, Vellacott's entranced figures in a landscape are based on people, places and situations she has seen. Her love of uncluttered composition was fired by long study of early Chinese and Japanese art; her liking for pure colour by her discovery of Byzantine and early Italian art, Matisse, Picasso and the Diaghilev ballet, and by work as a textile designer. The unique colour language emerging in Vellacott's mature art is articulated through hues both rich and slightly worn – as though touched by the Mediterranean sun beneath which she has often travelled. A luminous quality is enhanced by thin layers of oil applied to white board. Her eventual decision to paint on wooden panels, to retain maximum clarity of contour, recalls icons much admired from early visits to the Victoria and Albert Museum.

That Elisabeth Vellacott's subtle, contemplative art springs from direct observation of nature can be seen most clearly in her many landscape drawings – always produced on the spot. Some are notes for paintings; others are finished works, where scores of tiny pencil, graphite or chalk strokes delicately detail the features of tree and river bank. Such concentrated line and shading is expertly set against unmarked spaces of paper, capturing the feel of the environment in which she lives. Recurring themes have been the orchard around her home – most of which was sold to a speculative builder in the early 1960s, and bulldozed for housing – and the moat enclosing Lucy Boston's magical Norman manor ('Green Knowe' in her much-loved children's books).

A sense of tranquillity in this work is reflected in the gentle contours of the countryside. Gardens merge with orchards which combine with fields in a

Elisabeth Vellacott *People, Trees and Water*, 1985, oil on panel, 57 × 58cm.

domesticated world. People, perhaps more in touch with their roots than elsewhere, invest everyday tasks with the actions of ancient ceremony and ritual. History has been at work but time seems to be barely moving. The pictures themselves are produced extremely slowly. There is also a feeling that great knowledge has been amassed before any pigment or pencil is expended. (Elisabeth Vellacott had her first

Elisabeth Vellacott *Derelict Orchard*, 1963, charcoal, 50 × 62cm.

solo exhibition as late as 1968 – at The Minories, Colchester, then under the direction of Michael Chase.) There is no hint of strain or struggle. The determined painter, who was largely ignored until past the common retirement age, and who lost much of her early work when her Cambridge studio was bombed in 1942, offers an effortless vision. Like movements in a piece of music – concerts are favourite Vellacott subjects – the elements of her pictures blend gracefully into a harmonic whole.

Long before the arrival of Elisabeth Vellacott, untroubled landscapes beside the Ouse were recorded by a remarkable family of painters who, at the start of the 1880s, moved along the river from Bedford to Huntingdon.

The most gifted of three doctor's sons, **William Garden Fraser** (1856-1921) excelled at capturing the effects of shining and rippling water in scenes around Huntingdon, Houghton and St Ives. In the painting shown here, the art dealer and author Christopher Wood perceives 'an extraordinary, almost surrealistic stillness and intensity that . . . owes much to the Pre-Raphaelite vision.'

Nan Youngman *Ouse Washes*, 1974, watercolour, 28 × 35cm.

S PREADING like scissor blades for 20 miles from Earith, almost to Downham Market, the straight arms of the New and Old Bedford rivers enclose the Ouse Washes. In winter this marsh becomes a vast lake; an expanse around Welney, owned by the Wildfowl and Wetlands Trust, is turned into a natural airport, as hundreds of bewick and whooper swans taxi in after flights from Siberia. The wildness of this man-made world has been captured in a subtle watercolour by **Nan Youngman**.

Born in Kent in 1906, Nan Youngman got her first paintbox from her elder brother, Jack, who was killed in the First World War. Soon she discovered how to create sunsets by dropping watercolour on to wet paper, but only after studying at the Slade did she move through portraits and still life towards landscape painting. Her future career was also as an educationist: much influenced by her friend and teacher Marion Richardson, she directed Pictures for Schools exhibitions in London and Wales, from 1947 until 1969, and worked as a part-time county art adviser for Cambridgeshire. But all this time she also drew and painted prodigiously. Welsh mining communities and places around her home in Cambridge – shared with the sculptor Betty Rea – were favourite subjects for robust and resilient oils.

After Betty Rea's death in 1965, Nan Youngman moved to a house at Waterbeach, moored in a landscape of fen and dyke. Her later pictures, increasingly in watercolour, mirror her environment. Reducing in size, they see a removal of all but the most elemental features. A similarly haunting emptiness is reflected in her pictures of a stretch of the north Norfolk coast, around Brancaster.

The Fraser brothers took pains to hide their kinship in their work. William Garden Fraser preferred to sign himself W. F. Garden, Robert Winter Fraser chose to be known as Robert Winter and Robert Winchester Fraser used the name R. W. Fraser. But their paintings can now be seen to stem from a related viewpoint, with a strength far beyond period charm.

William Garden Fraser *Willows on the Ouse*, **1881, watercolour, 19 × 26cm (left).**

DURING THE first years of this century, the Ouse between Huntingdon and St Ives and the uncanny peace of England before the First World War were also captured in shimmering, impressionistic watercolours by **Frederick George Cotman** (1850-1920), nephew of the great John Sell Cotman.

He was born in Ipswich, where his father moved after the collapse of his Norwich silk mercer's business. Although at first he copied pictures by his uncle, and his cousins John Joseph and Miles Edmund Cotman – while a private pupil of W. Thompson Griffiths (then headmaster of the Ipswich School of Art) – F. G. Cotman later mirrored many of the more mainstream trends of Victorian art. As a student at the Royal Academy Schools, fully at ease with the prevailing fashion for realism in painting, he won four silver medals and a gold. Two visiting lecturers, the historical painter Frederick Leighton and the portraitist Henry Tanworth Wells, engaged him as an assistant on their own work; during holidays he helped the Colchester still life artist Edward Ladell. F. G. Cotman soon became a noted society portrait painter able, by the age of 29, to command a fee of 300 guineas for a full-length likeness. He also executed homely genre scenes and highly finished narrative pictures, in tune with the cloyingly sentimental taste of the times. Neither was he limited to a single medium – being elected a member of both the Royal Institute of Painters in Water-colours and the Royal Institute of Oil Painters. A wife and six children were supported on his success.

By the late 1880s F. G. Cotman was painting mostly landscapes. He travelled widely, but was preoccupied with the light and atmosphere of his native East Anglia. Rainbows, hazy effects of brilliant sunshine and early morning or evening mists along the region's waterways inspired some of his freest and finest work. In 1897, after a long period in London, the artist moved to Lowestoft, to enjoy his favourite sport of yachting. Two years later he was elected president of the Ipswich Fine Art Club. By 1902 he had acquired a studio at Hemingford Grey, and three years later he settled in the nearby market town of St Ives. From his Fenland base, he continued to work and exhibit until well into the First World War when, with failing eyesight, he retired to live near the sea at Felixstowe.

Anxious to push himself to the limit, the young F. G. Cotman had once seemed in danger of burning out. As a student he had complained of a 'peculiar feeling round my heart', which was diagnosed as palpitations brought on by nervousness. But any tendency to mental instability – which had dogged his uncle and more than one of his cousins – did not develop. The artist proved himself a versatile technician, with the tenacity and talent to emerge from the shadow of his famous forebear.

Frederick George Cotman *Morning Mist, Hemingford Grey*, 1904, pencil and watercolour, 29 × 45cm.

Fenland is a vast plain of fertile peat – a grid of flat rectangles; an isolated world of outpost farms and villages. This area where Cambridgeshire, Norfolk and Lincolnshire meet has the forbidding beauty of something created at great cost. Once sea, then marsh, the Fens have been extracted from water to which they seek to return, and so a constant war is waged against flooding. Some local people are descended from fishermen who murdered Dutch engineer Vermuden's men in their drainage dykes. Here defiance competes with a gloom known as 'fen syndrome', which afflicted the Helpston poet John Clare. After his Fenland parish was drained and 'improved' in the early nineteenth century, he wrote: 'Inclosure like a buonaparte let not thing remain. It levelled every bush and tree and levelled every hill.' More than 150 years later, the bitingly satirical painter **Edward Burra** (1905-76), motoring through East Anglia, was much moved by the Fens. A resulting watercolour, while mocking an encroachment of bungalows and gnome-scattered gardens, portrayed sugar beet workers with rare sympathy. To Burra they seemed haunted by history and the harshness of their lot.

But this horizontal landscape is far from featureless. From road and railway line the solid forms of Ely and Peterborough cathedrals loom for miles. Barely less impressive landmarks are the churches ranged around Wisbech, the Fenland capital. In Clare's day, the grandeur of such architecture was recorded by John Sell Cotman, who set out to etch 'all the ornamented antiquities in Norfolk' in 1811. This century has seen **John Piper** (b. 1903) inspired to produce some of his finest work by the towers and spires of the Fens.

Few artists have been as widely travelled and versatile as Piper. He has designed stained-glass windows and pleasure gardens, theatre sets and firework displays, collages, pottery, furniture and book illustrations. He has written poems and guides, taken photographs and plotted television programmes. Much of his output – through oils, watercolours and etchings – has depicted buildings in a landscape. In everything he has displayed great enthusiasm. During the 1930s the Royal College of Art student met Braque at the Hampstead home of Jim Ede, later the founder of Kettles Yard in Cambridge, and caught the prevailing taste for abstraction. But even then he was reducing natural forms to their basic elements,

Edward Burra *Sugar Beet*, 1972, watercolour, 79 × 133cm.

however formalised they became. When he returned to a more obvious emphasis on a subject, some perceived treachery. In fact, his work has been joined by a continuous thread. Since re-evaluating Turner, Blake and Cotman, he has been an artist clearly in the English Romantic tradition; and, after his entry into the Church of England with his second wife in 1939, he has been at his most lyrical when depicting and decorating Anglican architecture.

Touring restlessly until serious illness in 1986, John Piper has recorded countless East Anglian monuments. Moreover, for many years he was the main set designer for the operas of Benjamin Britten (also creating the composer's memorial window at Aldeburgh); and during frequent visits to Aldeburgh and the surrounding area he has painted numerous church towers. Several such pictures are in triptych

John Piper
Tivetshall St. Mary, 1982, watercolour, 39 × 57cm (left).

John Piper
Terrington St. Clement, 1981, watercolour and mixed media, 57 × 79cm (below).

form (for instance *Lexfield, Lavenham and Darsham,* a watercolour of 1965). People rarely figure in this artist's work, but he has been touched most powerfully by what he has described as 'the medieval builders using majestically the Fens as a plinth – the best plinth for sculptural architecture in the whole country'.

Stone from the Ancaster quarries near Sleaford produced most Fenland towers and rain or vicious 'fen blow' winds then amended the work of masons. Cotman, sensitive to the special character of beauty in decay, painted many medieval ruins. Piper has traced the Norwich School master's footsteps across the Fens, and focused on the area's crumbling churches. 'From a distance their upright outlines are straight enough, but straight and upright with an unaccountable richness', he wrote in *Architectural Review* in 1940.

'Closer, they are seen to have dissolved away round their stratified core of stone as if they had been under water or had been sand-blasted by a vague and artistic mechanic.' Serrations in the surface of each block had become as deep as the gaps made in the joints by the weather, making the substance of the wall a sculptural whole. Piper continued: 'It is incised and pitted by the weather; lichen stars or spreads it with yellow and gold; the mouldings of windows and arcades have become encrustations of curving ribs.' Such was the oneness of the churches, in relation to the level landscape, that the artist thought it 'fanciful but suggestive to imagine that these towers have been carved out of the level Fens, and the whole area of the land round them reduced in height by a hundred feet or so, leaving them solid and whole, like some Indian rock temples.'

John Piper *Wiggenhall St. Peter I,* **1983, watercolour, 50 × 67cm.**

John Piper *Wiggenhall St. Peter III,* **1983, watercolour and mixed media, 57 × 79cm.**

While writing this paean of praise, John Piper was seeing at close hand the destruction of great chunks of Britain's heritage. From April 1942, in response to an attack on historic Lubeck, Hitler ordered the Baedeker Raids against English cities and buildings of outstanding beauty. Norwich was targeted and Piper, an official war artist specialising in bomb damage, hurried all over the country to record the nation's architectural treasures before they were lost. A sense of urgency has remained in his work, and his appreciation of each building has been enhanced by a rare breadth of taste. Like his friend John Betjeman, this artist admires the best of the new as well as the old – pubs and palaces, cathedrals and humble churches.

Piper has highlighted the Fenland churches between Wisbech, King's Lynn and the Wash. In paint and in print he has waxed lyrical over Walsoken, West Walton, Walpole St Peter (thought by Betjeman to be the best church in England), the Wiggenhalls, the Tilneys and the Terringtons. He contends that such structures are more distinguished in mass than in detail, and has wrapped them in colour and light by turns murky and dazzling. A sense of drama may be bolstered by a low viewpoint and by patches of brilliant detail picked out of the gloom. Sketches may be worked up miles and years from the original site, but the finished picture retains an immediacy of response – pinning down season, weather and setting, to evoke the very spirit of time and place. Erratic effects are also true to nature, the artist has argued. 'Grey and gold and brown, and sometimes none of these, the towers are always afloat on a sea of Fen-green', he once wrote. 'Changeable skies give them bodies of infinitely varying light, sometimes pale and almost white against heavy clouds and shadowed marsh, sometimes burnished, sometimes glimmering, sometimes vivid, sometimes dim.'

INDEX OF ARTISTS

Mary Newcomb, *Four Guinea Fowl*

Charles Rennie Mackintosh, *Fritillaria*

ACKNOWLEDGEMENTS

1 Reproduced by courtesy of the School House Gallery, Wighton. **3** Rotherham Borough Council, Clifton Park Museum. **4** Courtesy Sotheby's, Sussex. **5** *top.* Ipswich Museums and Galleries, Ipswich Borough Council. *middle.* By courtesy of the Trustees of the Victoria and Albert Museum. *bottom.* Courtesy Crane Kalman Gallery. **7** Courtesy of the Cedric Morris Estate. **9** National Gallery of Scotland. **10** Ipswich Museums and Galleries, Ipswich Borough Council. **11** Norfolk Museums Service (Norwich Castle Museum). **12** Tate Gallery, London. **13** Norfolk Museums Service (Norwich Castle Museum). **14** North Woolwich Old Station Museum. **15** *top.* William Marler Gallery. *bottom.* Tryon Gallery. **16** By kind permission of Angela Verren-Taunt. **17** *bottom left.* Reproduced by courtesy of the School House Gallery, Wighton. *top and bottom right.* © Henry Moore Foundation 1990. Reproduced by kind permission of the Henry Moore Foundation. **18** *top.* Tate Gallery, London. *bottom.* Norfolk Museums Service (Norwich Castle Museum). **19** *bottom.* By kind permission of Trevor Castle. **20** Reproduced by kind permission of Luke Gertler and Dorothy Morland. **21** *top and bottom.* Reproduced by kind permission of Luke Gertler. **22** Collection of Hove Museum and Art Gallery. **23** Fitzwilliam Museum, Cambridge. **24** Courtesy of the Artist. **25** *bottom left.* Norfolk Museums Service (Great Yarmouth Museums). *middle.* Norfolk Museums Service (Norwich Castle Museum). **26/27** Norfolk Museums Service (Great Yarmouth Museums). **28** Rotherham Borough Council (Clifton Park Museum). **29** *top.* Mandell's Gallery. *bottom.* Tryon Gallery. **30** *top.* Judy Hines, Gallery 45, Norwich. *bottom.* By kind permission of Rodney Brangwyn. **31** *top and bottom.* Copyright Thomas Gibson Fine Art. **32** Norfolk Museums Service (Norwich Castle Museum), copyright Thomas Gibson Fine Art. **33** *top left and bottom right.* Norfolk Museums Service (Norwich Bridewell Museum). *bottom left.* Courtesy of the Artist and Norfolk Museums Service (Norwich Bridewell Museum). **34** Mandell's Gallery. **35** Private Collection. **36** Courtesy of Eastern Daily Press. **37/38** Courtesy of the Artist. **39** Courtesy of the Artist and Tate Gallery, London. **40/41** Courtesy of the Artist and Anthony d'Offay Gallery, London. **42** Austin Desmond Fine Art Limited. **43** Private Collection and courtesy Norfolk Museums Service (Great Yarmouth Museums). **44** *top.* Mandell's Gallery. *bottom.* Private Collection and courtesy Norfolk Museums Service (Great Yarmouth Museums). **45** Courtesy of Eastern Daily Press. **46** Norfolk Museums Service (Great Yarmouth Museums). **47** Dr M Connell and Norfolk Museums Service (Great Yarmouth Museums). **48/49/50** Norfolk Museums Service (Norwich Castle Museum). **51** Nottingham City Museums. **52/53** *bottom.* Courtesy Crane Kalman Gallery. **54** Courtesy Crane Kalman Gallery. **55** *top and bottom.* Courtesy of the Artist. **56** Courtesy of the Artist. **57** *left.* Courtesy of the Artist and the Arts Council Collection, South Bank Centre, London. *right.* Courtesy of the Artist and Annely Juda Fine Arts. **58** Courtesy of the Artist and Nigel Greenwood Gallery. **59** Aberdeen Art Gallery and Museums, Aberdeen City Arts Department. **60** *top.* Fitzwilliam Museum, Cambridge. *bottom.* Piccadilly Gallery. **61** *top.* Courtesy of Sotheby's. *bottom.* Courtesy Gillian Spencer and the New Grafton Gallery. **62** *top.* Bradford City Art Gallery. **63** *bottom.* Courtesy of Jane Martineau. **64** Fitzwilliam Museum, Cambridge. **65** *top.* Courtesy of Sotheby's. *bottom.* Browse and Darby. **66** Tate Gallery, London. **67** *top.* Fitzwilliam Museum, Cambridge. *bottom.* Ipswich Museums and Galleries, Ipswich Borough Council. **68** *left.* Courtesy of Sotheby's, Sussex. *right.* T and R Annan and Sons Ltd, Glasgow. **69** Private Collection. **70** Hunterian Art Gallery, University of Glasgow (Mackintosh Collection). 71/72/73 Private Collection. 74 Ipswich Museums and Galleries, Ipswich Borough Council. 75 *left.* Gillian Jason Gallery. *right.* By Courtesy of the Trustees of the Victoria and Albert Museum. 76 Ipswich Museums and Galleries, Ipswich Borough Council. 77 Gillian Jason Gallery. 78 Copyright John and Molly Hitchens and courtesy Geoffrey Robinson. 79 Courtesy Sheffield City Art Galleries and Angelica Garnett. 80 By kind permission of the Provost and Scholars of King's College, Cambridge and Angelica Garnett. 81 Norfolk Museums Service (Norwich Castle Museum) 82 *top.* By kind permission of Mr. and Mrs. Geoffrey Darke. *bottom.* Arts Council Collection, South Bank Centre, London. 83 *top.* Arts Council Collection, South Bank Centre, London. *bottom.* Courtesy of the Artist. 84 *top.* Norfolk Museums Service (Norwich Castle Museum) and courtesy of Rosemary Somerville. *bottom.* Courtesy of Stephen Reiss Gallery and Rosemary Somerville. 85 Norfolk Museums Service (Norwich Castle Museum) and courtesy of Rosemary Somerville. 86 *top.* Courtesy of Stephen Reiss Gallery and Rosemary Somerville. *bottom.* (Collection J. Neill). Courtesy of the Artist. 87/88/89/90/91 Ipswich Museums and Galleries, Ipswich Borough Council. 92/93 *bottom./*94 *right.* Redfern Gallery. 94 *left.* Reproduced by courtesy of the School House Gallery, Wighton. 95 Courtesy of the Cedric Morris Estate. 96 Courtesy of the Cedric Morris Estate and Austin Desmond Fine Art Limited. 97 *top.* Courtesy of the Artist. *bottom.* Courtesy of the Cedric Morris Estate and National Museum of Wales, Cardiff. 98 *top.* Courtesy of the Cedric Morris Estate and Sotheby's. *bottom.* Courtesy of the Artist. 99 *top.* Arts Council Collection, South Bank Centre, London. *bottom.* Courtesy of the Artist. 100 Austin Desmond Fine Art Limited. 101 *left.* Eastern Arts Association. *right.* Arts Council Collection, South Bank Centre, London. 102 *top.* Austin Desmond Fine Art Limited. 103 *top.* Courtesy Phoenix Galleries. *bottom.* Courtesy of the Artist and Browse and Darby. 104 Courtesy of the Artist and Browse and Darby. 105 Courtesy of the Artist. 106 *top.* By kind permission of Lionel Edwards' family and courtesy Sotheby's. 106 *bottom.* By kind permission of Lionel Edwards' family, British Sporting Art Trust and Tryon Gallery. 107 Courtesy Sotheby's, New York and copyright Sir Alfred Munnings Art Museum, Dedham, Essex. 108 Norfolk Museums Service (Norwich Castle Museum), copyright Sir Alfred Munnings Art Museum, Dedham, Essex. 109 W H Patterson. 110 Arthur Ackermann and Son Limited, copyright Sir Alfred Munnings Art Museum, Dedham, Essex. 111 *top.* Norfolk Museums Service (Norwich Castle Museum), copyright Sir Alfred Munnings Art Museum, Dedham, Essex. *bottom.* Ipswich Museums and Galleries, Ipswich Borough Council. 112 *left.* Tate Gallery, London. 112 *right/*113/114 The Artistic Trustee. 115/116 *left and right.* Fine Art Society. 117/118 *top and bottom.* By kind permission of Jane Smith and courtesy Sotheby's. 119 By courtesy of the Trustees of the Victoria and Albert Museum. 120 Fine Art Society. 121 Towner Art Gallery and Local History Museum, Eastbourne. 122/123 Fine Art Society. 124/125 Arts Council Collection, South Bank Centre, London and Dr Anne Weightman. 126/127 Courtesy of the Artist and Redfern Gallery, London. 128 Courtesy of Elisabeth Ayrton. 129 Courtesy of Georgina Barker. 130/131 *top and bottom.* Private Collection. 133 Fitzwilliam Museum, Cambridge. 134/135/136 *top.* Courtesy of the Artist. 136 *bottom.* Courtesy of the Artist and John and Sue Stanford. 137 *top.* Christopher Wood Collection. *bottom.* Norfolk Museums Service (Norwich Castle Museum). 138 Courtesy of the Lefevre Gallery. 139 *top and bottom,* 140, 141 Courtesy of the Artist. 144 Reproduced by kind permission of Shell UK Ltd.

Duncan Grant *St. Ives, Huntingdon,* oil on canvas. Reproduced in 1932 as a poster for the Shell Company's 'Everywhere You Go' series.

While I take full responsibility for any error in this volume, information and inspiration have been trawled from a wide pool.

I am much indebted to the help and hospitality of Margaret Mellis, Prunella Clough, Elisabeth Vellacott, Iris and Nigel Weaver, Michael Chase and Valerie Thornton, Alfred and Diana Cohen, Mary and Godfrey Newcomb, Colin Self, Basil Lawrence, Prof. John Ball and the late Dr. Gordon Hargreaves.

For further assistance I would like to thank John Allen, Janice Baldwin, Emily Barker, Georgina Barker, Sebastian Barker, the late Edward Bawden, Philip Bawden, Quentin Bell, Hugh Belsey, Chloe Bennett, John Bensusan-Butt, Roger Billcliffe, the Rev. Canon David Bishop, Ronald Blythe, Roger Bristow, Michael Buhler, Nancy Carline, Dawn and Trevor Castle, Joanna Cherry, Anthony Collins, Olive Cook, Tim Corbett, East Anglian Daily Times, Eastern Daily Press, Damian Eaton, Dr. Robert Fountain, Ann Garrould, Luke Gertler, Eric Goodwin, Sophie Gurney, Richard Harrison, Ivor Hook, Bobby Hunt, Marjorie Jenkins, Brian Johnston, Prue Loftus, Simon Loftus (on Harry Becker), Dr. Patrick Luffman, Jean Macalpine, Michael MacLeod, Dr. Hugh Maingay, Jane Martineau, the Rev. Thelma Melbourne, Dorothy Morland, Michael Parkin, Stephen Reiss, Bryan Robertson, Peyton Skipwith, Frances Spalding, Shirin Spencer, Unity Spencer, Gillian Spencer, Anne Stevens (on Claughton Pellew), staff of the Tate Gallery and the Royal Academy, Michael Ward, Owen Waters, Norma Watt, Lady Joan Zuckerman.

In addition, I wish to express my gratitude to Andrew Dodds for his invaluable advice, my excellent editor Michelle Jarrold, designer Geoff Staff, and Ian McIntyre for making the project possible.